DRUG

DEPENDENCE

DRUG

DEPENDENCE

Social Regulation
and Treatment Alternatives

By Carl N. Edwards

With a Foreword by The Honorable Franklin N. Flaschner

Published in association with John A. Calhoun
and the Justice Resource Institute

Jason Aronson, New York

LIBRARY OF CONGRESS CATALOGING IN PUBLICATION DATA
Edwards, Carl N
    Drug dependence: social regulation and treatment
alternatives.
    Published in 1973 under title: Justice administration
and drug dependence: issues and alternatives.
    Bibliography: p.
    1. Drug abuse. 2. Narcotics, Control of.
3. Drug abuse—Treatment. I. Title.   [DNLM: 1. Drug
abuse. 2. Drug addiction. 3. Drug and narcotic
control. WM270 E26d 1974]
HV5801.E39   1974   362.2'93   73-17739
ISBN 0-87668-117-8

Designed by Raymond Solomon

Manufactured in the United States of America

iv

Contents

Acknowledgments

Preparation of this book was supported, in part, by Grant No. 73-ED-01-0010 from the United States Department of Justice. The authors wish to express their appreciation to Robert J. Coakley, Matthew P. Dumont, Sherwin Feinhandler, Alan Fisch, Louisa P. Howe, Vernon D. Patch, James F. Patterson, and George E. Vaillant for their cooperation and assistance. We are particularly indebted to Mariam Maxwell for her major contribution to the research and preparation of this study. Final responsibility for the book and its contents rests, of course, with the authors.

Foreword

Both the fascination and the fright in public attitudes toward drugs have been ageless. Escapes or trips away from wearisome routine can be thrilling and scary. If the escapee or tripper gets into trouble, he may evoke sympathy, but at the same time his conduct may be menacing and invoke recrimination. In the extreme he may even end up a scapegoat. We really do not know very much about the magnetism of drugs and we do not understand the seesawing of our reactions between helpfulness and repression toward those who abuse drugs and use them illegally.

If the law and its servants, the judges, mirror changing values in society, they cannot avoid reflecting its confusion. Few areas of the law and its administration have appeared more confusing than that of dealing with drug-dependent persons. As has been pointed out so vividly by Dr. Karl Menninger in *The Crime of Punishment*, by Justice Marvin Frankel in *Criminal Sentences*, and by so many other responsible critics of our criminal justice system, there are cavernous inadequacies in the ways we deal with offenders. While the unknowns of human behavior, both on the part of the offenders and the offended, contribute significantly to our failures in dealing with all offenders, there is a uniquely intense degree of the unknown about drug offenders.

One reflection of the confusion about a public issue is the quantity of books and articles written on the subject. In the field of drugs it has been almost as if the writers are trying to fight the pills with pages. Heightened public interest must be fed. Hopefully, in the process of wrestling with problems, public understanding and knowledge emerge.

As a literary wrestling match with the basic problems underlying drug dependence, this work may have no equal. The authors have devoted themselves to a scholarly analysis of drug dependence as viewed from the disciplines of human behavior, medicine, and law. Perhaps because of the authors' backgrounds and perspective, the direction of their scholarship is fresh and independent. Perhaps for the same reason, the reader may find their analysis uncompromisingly thorough and at times demanding. Not everyone will agree with their conclusions, but the serious reader should be rewarded with expanding and deepening perceptions of the problem of drug dependence in modern society.

Being hard on drug sellers and easy on users is an oversimplified judicial response to the problem. Admittedly, big-time sellers, whenever they are caught and convicted, deserve the stiffer penalties provided by law. However, most convicted sellers are not big time and practically all of them are users. Another oversimplified response is that the increase in crimes of violence is due to drug abuse. Of course there has been a dramatic increase in crimes of violence, but the causes of violence focus on social forces, of which drug use is only a correlate. Judges who have been influenced by pleas of sympathy for a defendant convicted of a violent crime because he takes drugs are now looking more closely at this defendant's profile and discovering that he is frequently a person who was as prone to violence before as after he became a drug user. Both violence and drugs are a part of modern culture. Drug treatment alone is seldom an adequate response.

Even in those cases where drug treatment is appropriate, judges and probation officers are confused about the results. The oversimplification here is that referral to a responsible drug treatment program is bound to succeed, or conversely, if it does not succeed in a number of cases, such referrals should not be made. The establishment of drug-screening and advisory boards to work with the probation department and the judge is one technique that assists the court in its ongoing supervision of drug-dependent offenders.

However fair, responsive, and professional are the services of the court and the social agencies, the drug-dependent offender must be deemed responsible for his or her actions. Only incompetence by reason of mental illness or retardation raises questions of involuntary civil commit-

Foreword

ment. In these instances the defendant is no different from any other legally incompetent or dangerously mentally ill person. In all other respects, the drug user, as the authors of this work conclude, *are* subject to the just claims of others.

Understanding the nature of drug use and gaining a perspective on where it fits in modern culture should assist in clarifying proper medical, legal, and social responses to the problems of drug-dependent persons. As this work demonstrates, however, we have to make a patient and studious review of how these separate disciplines have responded in order to distill an integrated response which is so desperately needed.

Franklin N. Flaschner,
Chief Justice

District Courts of Massachusetts
West Newton, Massachusetts
June 28, 1973

Preface

By their nature, major social issues tend to become inextricably tied to the human, social, and political climate of their time. As an issue captures the attention and concern of the public and as the public struggles to respond, the issue becomes a focal point against which every other human need is assessed. It is during such a period that objectives become most easily confused and the temptations of a readily available expedient are most compelling. These are truly times that demand the very best from our social institutions.

Of our current social issues, few have as many different and competing perspectives as the issue of drug abuse. Each of our social institutions has a clear stake and defined responsibility in relation to drug abuse, yet each, by virtue of its own history, tradition, and individual mandate, tends to view the issue differently. These differences are unfortunate, in that they tend to mask common objectives, but at the same time many differences are a realistic and essential response to the unique responsiblities of each institution. This book represents an attempt to examine and place in perspective both the common objectives and separate responsibilities of those who, by the nature of their response, will determine the course of drug abuse in our society.

It is not the intent of this report to prescribe solutions to social problems; both the definition of and response to issues that affect society must ultimately find their resolution in the actions of the members of that society. At the same time, it is not our intent to present here a blueprint for professional drug programs. Effective and responsible programs must and will be developed to respond to the challenges before us. It has become apparent, however, that the challenges of contemporary drug abuse demand an unprecedented level of mutual understanding and cooperation between social institutions. The way we will respond to the issue of drugs in our society must rest in the hands of the men and women who shape and build those institutions.

We are confident that every reader appreciates the difficult and shifting demands of this area of public service. Above all, we share a common concern that the recipients of our services will be treated as individuals and that their rights and responsibilities will not be unduly subjected to the whims of a changing social climate. Our intent here is to examine the issues we confront and the alternatives we face. We offer not a final word but a point of departure, a perspective and a premise from which we may work together to meet our common objectives. We invite your response and participation in this process.

CNE
JC

Chapter 1

Drugs and Society: The Human Dilemma

". . . and of our pleasant vices
Make instruments to plague us."

—*King Lear*

During the past decade, drug abuse has found its way to a position among the top ten American social issues. At the heart of the issue are four basic observations. First, the use of self-administered psychoactive drugs has increased to the point where virtually all areas and segments of the population are potentially exposed to them. Second, in most instances, use of these drugs is of no demonstrable medicinal value, and the correlates of use, if any, are in the direction

1

of reducing the level of productivity of the user. Third, such use without benefit of medical sanction and supervision is, in most instances, in violation of the law. Finally, increased usage, coupled with its illegality, has resulted in a situation where demand is satisfied through illegal means which offer neither cost nor quality control. These factors combined result in the diversion of increased human and financial resources to illegal channels.

These basic observations have resulted in far-reaching public and professional concern. The communication media have devoted increasing attention to the coverage of drug abuse, and the full resources of the professional and academic communities have been mobilized in an effort to research and clarify the nature, extent, and cause of the drug phenomenon. These efforts have resulted, ironically, in the production of more publications related to drug abuse than there are known drug addicts registered with the Federal Bureau of Narcotics. Now, as we turn to this literature for information and direction, it becomes apparent that there are virtually no facts, conclusions, or items of terminology that a professional consensus subscribes to. The President's Commission on Law Enforcement and the Administration of Justice, after examining the best available evidence, arrived at a recommendation that could have been written as easily at any other time in our nation's history:

Research should be undertaken devoted to early action on the further development of a sound and effective framework of regulatory and criminal laws with respect to dangerous drugs. In addition, research and educational programs concerning the effects of such drugs should be undertaken. [1967, p. 216]

A frequently consulted medical text provides the following explanation of drug abuse:

The use of drugs may provide a means of expressing hostility toward individuals or society or a way of self-punishment. Psychiatric factors are of prime importance, and all addicts can be shown to have personality defects, which, so far as can be judged from the history, antedate the addiction. [Isbell, 1963, p. 1,746]

The same text goes on to recommend:

One should not attempt to treat narcotic addiction on an outpatient basis. . . . All patients should engage in a program of individual occupational and recreational therapy that should provide them with an opportunity to carry out at least eight hours of useful, productive work daily. . . . [p. 1,749]

By contrast, Andrew Weil, a physician and former drug researcher, left the field of medical research after concluding that ". . . a desire to alter consciousness periodically is an innate, normal drive analogous to hunger or the sexual drive." [1972, p. 66]

A similar conclusion prompted Martin M. Katz, Chief of the Clinical Research Branch of the National Institute of Mental Health's Extramural Research Programs, to state in

3

a popular psychological publication: "What this country needs is a safe, five-cent intoxicant." [1971, p. 28]

A review of the history of intoxicants [Blum, 1970a; Brecher, 1972] tends to confirm this view. All evidence in this area indicates that the use of intoxicants developed independently in virtually all cultures and that the practice dates back to the dawn of recorded history. Again, to quote Weil:

> . . . many Americans seem to feel that the contemporary drug scene is something new, qualitatively different from what has gone before. There is no evidence that a greater percentage of Americans are taking drugs, only that younger Americans prefer illegal drugs like marijuana and hallucinogens to alcohol. Therefore, those who insist that everyone is suddenly taking drugs apparently regard alcohol as being outside the category of drugs. Drug taking is bad. We drink alcohol. Therefore, alcohol is not a drug. [1972, p. 65]

The parallel between illicit drug use and alcohol or other forms of illicit drug use is frequently, and appropriately, drawn [Fort, 1969; Brecher, 1972]. Three-fourths of all American adults, representing all social and economic groups, use alcohol. Americans purchase $18 billion worth of alcohol and $9 billion worth of tobacco annually. In addition, approximately half of all American adults report having used prescription or over-the-counter psychoactive drugs [Balter and Levine, 1969]. Estimates of marijuana usage vary widely, but most agree that the practice exists

4

not only among adolescents [King, 1969; Defleur and Garrett, 1970; Mizner, Barter, and Werme, 1970; Hager, Vener, and Steward, 1971], but adults as well [McGlothlin, Arnold, and Rowan, 1970; Brecher, 1972]. Stanley Yolles, then Director of the National Institute of Mental Health, placed the number of Americans who had used marijuana one or more times as of 1969 at between eight and twelve million. Other authorities place the current estimate at several times that number.[1]

The literature also fails to provide consistent evidence of the consequences of such drug use. Harvard psychiatrist Lester Grinspoon, who has provided perhaps the most thorough and systematic review of marijuana use, concludes:

> . . . marijuana is a relatively safe intoxicant that is not addicting, does not in and of itself lead to the use of harder drugs, is not criminogenic, and does not lead to sexual excess, and the evidence that it may lead to personality deterioration and psychosis is quite unconvincing. . . . [1971, p. 323]

Indeed, the case has even been made that narcotic addicts can and often do lead normal and productive lives [Brecher, 1972, pp. 33-41]. Fifty years ago a United States Public Health official, Dr. Lawrence Kolb, investigated the effects of narcotic addiction and their relationship to crime and anti-social behavior. His conclusions remain widely supported by contemporary researchers:

Drugs and Society: The Human Dilemma

All preparations of opium capable of producing addiction inhibit aggressive impulses and make psychopaths less likely to commit crimes of violence. . . . Habitual criminals are psychopaths and psychopaths are abnormal individuals who, because of their abnormality, are especially liable to become addicts. Addiction is only an incident in their delinquent careers, and the crimes they commit are not precipitated by the drugs they take. [1925a, p. 88]

The view that drug laws themselves are responsible for the crimes they are intended to prevent also enjoys wide support:

As the law stands . . . the addict user almost inevitably turns to crime to support his habit at inflated black market prices. Typical and notorious are the robberies by heroin users which amount to $3 billion a year in New York and . . . this does not include the cost of protective devices . . . that city dwellers are obliged to install. . . . The law defines the drug user as a criminal and a deviant, and he will frequently conform to this image. [Zinberg and Robertson, 1972, pp. 204-205]

In light of these questions, it is not surprising to find that such diverse groups as the Joint Committee of the Bar Association and the American Medical Association on Narcotic Drugs [Eldridge, 1962] and William Buckley Jr.'s *National Review* [Cowan, 1972] have adopted positions in support of the liberalization of our present drug laws. The prospect of modification in the legal structure surrounding drug use has, however, created a broad spectrum of con-

6

cern among both professionals and the general public. Consistent with this concern is the wide support given the President's Commission on Law Enforcement and the Administration of Justice in their recommendation that:

> The enforcement staff of the Bureau of Narcotics should be materially increased. Some part of the added personnel should be used to design and execute a long-range intelligence effort aimed at the upper echelons of the illicit drug traffic. [1967, p. 220]

One explanation for the public concern with drug regulation, and particularly the seemingly inconsistent attitudes toward alcohol and marijuana, is voiced by Grinspoon:

> In this country alcohol is an agent which lubricates the wheels of commerce and catalyzes social intercourse. Marijuana is considered to be "just for fun" and, therefore, is in conflict with powerful vestiges of the Protestant ethic which demands self-control (except at specifically prescribed times, when the restraints are lowered briefly), hard work, rationality, order, moderation, and future-oriented planning. [1971, p. 333]

The point is well taken and raises issues which we shall return to later. The statement itself, however, is inconsistent with the facts surrounding our use of alcohol and other "legal" drugs. Joel Fort has pointed out that:

> More than half of those in our jails and prisons for crimes against the person or property, including murders, rape,

theft, burglary, and embezzlement, committed these crimes in association with (excessive) alcohol use. Many suicides and accidental deaths involve heavy consumption of alcohol, often in combination with a biologically identical drug, barbiturates. Between 50 percent and 70 percent of the almost 55,000 deaths and 2.5 million severe injuries each year from automobile accidents involve or are caused by alcohol. [1969, p. 37]

In a country that incurs more death and injury as a result of the abuse of its "legal" drugs than to war and national defense, it is difficult to attribute motivations to self-control, rationality, and moderation. While the attempt to prohibit alcohol under the Eighteenth Amendment can only be viewed as a total failure, the regulation of alcohol abuse following its repeal under the Twenty-first Amendment can hardly be viewed as a success. Despite the optimistic argument in favor of drug legalization, the American public is deeply aware of the abuse potential of those same drugs, legal and illegal. While the physiological consequences of drug use, including narcotics and hallucinogens, have been widely debated [Brecher, 1972], the public remains most directly concerned with human consequences. The public's concern—while complex, contradictory, and often self-serving—nevertheless includes a strong desire to protect itself and future generations from the costs, both human and financial, of drug abuse.

Perhaps the most persuasive evidence of the severe consequences of drug use, in the public view, has been provided by professionals working in the area of rehabilitation.

Until recently the therapeutic approaches to the treatment of drug dependency which appeared to offer the greatest promise were those based on the self-help model [Dumont, 1972]. While commonly associated with the treatment of narcotics addicts, the model is essentially the same as that often used with alcohol, marijuana, and other social drugs. The approach had its origins in the formation, during the late 1950s, of an "anti-addiction society" commonly known as "Synanon" [Yablonsky, 1965]. The Synanon phenomenon gained wide popularity and led to the formation of a nationwide network of "therapeutic communities" patterned after the original organization in Santa Monica, California.

At first, the Synanon approach was considered a "cure." By the mid-1960s, however, Synanon itself began modifying its claims. In 1971 Charles Dederich, the founder, told reporters:

> We once had the idea of "graduates." This was a sop to social workers and professionals who wanted us to say that we were producing "graduates." I always wanted to say to them "a person with this fatal disease will have to live here all his life." A few, but very few, have gone out and made it. . . . Roughly one in ten has stayed clean outside for as much as two years.[2]

The disease concept of addiction has been gaining ground for the last decade. The best-known proponents of this position are the husband-and-wife team of Vincent Dole and Marie Nyswander. Dole, a researcher in metabolic disease, collaborated with Nyswander in the introduction of a metabolic disease theory of addiction:

> The new evidence provided by the results of maintenance treatment strongly suggests that the "addict traits" are a consequence, not a cause, of addiction and demonstrates that a substantial number of addicts can be rehabilitated on a medical program. [Dole and Nyswander, 1967]

The "maintenance treatment" is methadone maintenance [Dole and Nyswander, 1965]. With a disease concept of addiction, the way has been opened for a return to the medical model of treatment for drug dependence. Methadone maintenance is rapidly becoming the treatment of choice for heroin addiction, and an impressive array of evidence has been compiled to support its effectiveness in dealing with the symptoms of addiction and addiction-related criminal activity [Patch, 1972].

The medical model offers solutions that are, however, far from perfect. When first developed, heroin itself was considered an effective substitute for morphine in the treatment of morphine addiction. The prospect of history simply repeating itself has been raised by many observers. This and other objections have been discussed by Lennard, Epstein, and Rosenthal [1972] in a paper regarded by many as the best critique of the methadone approach. One point in particular must be seriously considered:

> The decision to use methadone on a large scale supports, and indeed reinforces, a drug-oriented approach to the solu-

tion of social and personal problems. Such a decision . . . may have untoward consequences for large groups of persons not yet introduced into the use and misuse of psychoactive drugs, in that it legitimizes the use of drugs to regulate the disturbances of social life. [1972, p. 882]

The most vehement criticisms of this medical approach have been raised not by professional opponents of methadone maintenance, but by the potential recipients [Heyman, 1972]. Ron Clark, Director of RAP, Inc., a drug-free rehabilitation program, said in a statement prepared jointly with the Medical Committee for Human Rights:

[methadone maintenance is] creating a new industry designed to enrich the medical profession, as well as to tranquilize young black people, rather than giving them the survival education they desperately need.[3]

The concept of addiction as an illness has, however, gained wide support and formed the basis for the Supreme Court's landmark decision in the case of *Robinson v. California*.[4] In their review of the case, the Court held that narcotic addiction is an illness, not a crime. As such, the California statute which made the status of addiction a criminal offense imposed a "cruel and unusual punishment" and was in violation of the Fourteenth Amendment. This interpretation at first appears consistent with a view held by many opponents of the criminalization of drug use, namely that addiction is a crime without a victim [Schur, 1965] and

11

should not fall under the purview of the criminal law. This view has been regularly advanced by users of hallucinogens on the grounds that the individual has the right to determine what will or will not be introduced into his or her own body.

The Supreme Court, however, made it clear that it was not sanctioning the use of illegal and dangerous drugs:

> In the interest of discouraging the violations of [drug laws] . . . , or in the interest of the general health and welfare of its inhabitants, a State might establish a program of compulsory treatment for those addicted to narcotics. Such a program of treatment might require periods of involuntary confinement. And penal sanctions might be imposed for failure to comply with established treatment procedures.

The phrase "civil commitment for narcotics addiction," with its beneficent sound and clear medical overtones, resurrected the heated and controversial emotions that surround the issue of drug abuse. California was among the first to adopt a civil commitment program for narcotic addiction and, inevitably, the spirit of the program was the topic of considerable debate. In particular, the prospect of a civil commitment program was viewed by many as effectively nullifying the deterrent value of narcotics laws. The result was a compromise.

In describing the operation and objectives of the California civil commitment programs, the then Director of the Department of Correction summarized the operation in these terms:

. . . [the addict] has three choices: he may stay clean through the efforts we are going to make together; he may stay locked up, and I assure you that we can do this; or, he can get out of the state.[5]

This statement was sufficient to incur the wrath of any serious civil libertarian. The result was a systematic attack on the concept of civil commitment [Aronowitz, 1967; Kramer, 1970]. Counsel for the American Civil Liberties Union summarized their concern:

We have not fought [to extract addicts from jail] only to have them involuntarily committed for an even longer period of time, with no assurance of appropriate rehabilitative help and treatment. . . . The euphemistic name "civil commitment" can easily hide nothing more than permanent incarceration. . . . I would caution those who might rush headlong to adopt civil commitment procedures and remind them that just as difficult legal problems exist there as with ordinary jail sentences.[6]

The Supreme Court decision in *Robinson v. California* raises additional issues as to the scope of the interpretation. These issues have been discussed by S. Carter McMorris:

the . . . view, which I espouse . . . is that *Robinson* applies to acts incidental to narcotics addiction as well. The most notable of these is the possession of the narcotic used in the course of the addiction, but these acts also might include derivative ones, such as the sale of drugs or the commission of secondary crimes to support addiction. . . . Any federal prohibition of a state's punishing a "status" equally pro-hibits the state's punishing as an "act" conduct which is an inevitable and endemic attribute of the status. [1970, p. 43]

McMorris goes on to state:

Narcotics addiction is a form of insanity, rendering the subject incapable of committing the offense alleged, so that it is a denial of due process and equal protection of the laws to punish him for the offense. . . .

Our current "liberal" approach . . . only scratches the sur-face of a real and effective program, in which causes will be dealt with harshly, while the victim of disorganized social conditions, who finds the violation of law natural to him in his environment, will be treated with humanity and under-standing. The battle must be fought not by an attack on the criminal, but by treatment of him, and an attack on all fronts against those social determinants—poverty, igno-rance and insecurity—that lead to crime. [1970, pp. 45, 48]

If drug addiction is a disease, McMorris requires us to examine the nature of that disease. All medical theories aside, few definitions have been able to go beyond that of Maurer and Vogel:

Although we commonly speak of drug addiction as a dis-ease, it is more properly a symptom of disease rooted in social and economic conditions which tend to create dis-satisfaction, unhappiness, conflict, tension, and strife in the minds and souls of human beings.[7]

14

Drugs and Society: The Human Dilemma

On the basis of the collective literature, it is possible to conclude that drug use is a normal, age-old, and relatively harmless pursuit, associated with an incurable disease having grave social consequences, which can be neither punished nor involuntarily treated. If this were correct, it could only support the popular belief in the failure of our institutions, including law and medicine, to respond to the challenge of major social issues. Before we accept this conclusion, we must consider that social issues seldom fall simply within the domain of law, medicine, or any other single discipline. While further research is both necessary and justified, it is unlikely that future scientific or technological discoveries will provide the answer to the fundamental issues we now face. By definition, social issues are inextricably tied to deep and profound human dilemmas. Recognition of this fact is the first step in meeting the challenge before us.

Notes

1. Testimony in Narcotics Legislation hearings before the Subcommittee to Investigate Juvenile Delinquency of the Committee on the Judiciary, U.S. Senate, 91st Congress, 1st Session, September 17, 1969.

2. Quoted in Brecher (1972, p. 98).

3. Quoted in the *Journal of the Addiction Research Foundation*, 1972, *1*(7), p. 1.

4. *Robinson v. California*, 370 U.S. 660 (1962).

5. Quoted in Kramer (1970, pp. 1–2).

6. Quoted in *Powell v. Texas*, 392 U.S. 514 (1968).

7. Quoted in Aronowitz (1967, p. 417).

Chapter 2

Psychiatry and the Law

"How small, of all that human hearts endure, That part that laws or kings can cause or cure."

—*Oliver Goldsmith*

Over half a century has passed since J.B. Watson proclaimed that "only the sick or psychopaths . . . commit crimes . . . The fate of those individuals should be in medical (psychiatric) hands. . . . Naturally, such a view does away completely with criminal law . . . the criminal lawyer . . . legal precedent, and with the courts" [1930, pp. 185-86]. Our administration of justice in the United States has not reached this point, but psychiatry and the law have had a long and often uneasv historical relationship. In 1908 Louis Brandeis defended Oregon's women's labor protection law before the Supreme Court, through reference to social and medical documentation.[1] Today behavioral scientists look with pride to the 1954 Supreme Court recognition of psychological studies in arriving at the decision that school segregation was inherently harmful.[2]

More often than not, however, law and psychiatry view each other with guarded optimism or mutual distrust. In one study, more than 40 percent of the lawyers surveyed voted against the proposition that it is worthwhile to obtain a psychiatrist's help when someone begins to act strangely; and more than two-thirds endorsed secrecy about family mental illness [Overholser, 1953, p. 133]. In part, this phenomenon can be traced to a traditional conflict between the behavioral scientist's and the clinician's identification and concern with the understanding and treatment of the individual, and the legal profession's concern and responsibility fot the protection and regulation of society.

Among primitive men, not only human beings, but animals and inanimate objects as well, were held morally responsible for their actions and the supposed consequences of those actions. This view passed quickly, however, and the criminal law gradually evolved one of its most fundamental propositions: that no person can be held criminally liable and punishable for an illegal act unless he has *mens rea*, or criminal intent. While the concept of *mens rea* did not exist in anything like its modern sense until the twelfth century,

18

. . . the intent of the defendant seems to have been a material factor, even from the very earliest times in determining the extent of punishment. It was manifestly unjust that the man who accidentally killed with no intention of doing harm should suffer the extreme penalty of death. True, he might have to pay the *wer*, the fixed price to buy off the vengeance of the victim's kin, but beyond that he should not be punished. [Sayre, 1932, pp. 981-982]

The concept of *mens rea* can, however, be a misleading one. For one thing, it has never been true that *mens rea* refers to a stable, concrete entity. Its meaning and interpretation has changed continually throughout history. More importantly, *mental illness, in and of itself, has never been a sole determinant of the degree of criminal responsibility*. Every test of responsibility yet devised has sought to separate one group of the mentally ill from the rest so as to excuse them alone; the test of responsibility simply consists of the criteria which are to be used to do this. In addition to the presence of mental illness, there are always other requirements to be met.

The twelfth century saw an increasing awareness and concern for the concept of moral guilt. Bracton, a thirteenth-century jurist and clergyman strongly influenced by the canon law, wrote:

. . . take away the will and every act will be indifferent because your state of mind gives meaning to your act, and a crime is not committed unless the intent to injure intervene . . . this is in accordance with what might be said of the infant or the madman, since the innocence of design protects the one and the lack of reason in committing the act excuses the other.[3]

For Bracton a "madman" was one who lacked in "mind and reason, one who is not far removed from the brutes." By modern standards, only the most severe psychotic states could be included in this definition of insanity. Not until Freud introduced the concept of the unconscious during the early twentieth century were tests of criminal responsibility expanded to include other than cognitive defects. In fact, the definition of insanity changed very little until the eighteenth century.

In 1760 the English case of Earl Ferrer gave rise to the "good and evil" test, which is still a part of contemporary United States law. In the words of the Crown's counsel:

> . . . if there be only a partial degree of insanity, mixed with a partial degree of reason; not a full and complete use of reason, but a competent use of it, sufficient to have restrained those passions, which produced the crime . . . then, upon the fact of the offense provided, the judgement of the law must take place. . . . The question, therefore, must be asked; is the noble prisoner at the bar to be acquitted from the guilt of murder, on account of insanity? . . . Was he under the power of it, at the time of the offense committed? Could he, did he, at the time, distinguish between good and evil?[4]

The decision popularly known as the *McNaghten Rule* was a logical extension of the Ferrer case. Daniel McNaghten, apparently suffering from delusions of prosecution, was convinced that the British Prime Minister, Robert Peel, was among his enemies. In 1843, during an attempt on Peel's life, he shot and killed Peel's private secretary, whom he mistook for Peel. The jury, largely on the medical testimony of a Dr. E.R. Monro, reached a verdict of "not guilty, on the ground of insanity."

Queen Victoria and the press were incensed by what seemed to them to be an outlandish permissiveness on the part of the courts. The McNaghten incident followed a rash of assassination attempts on the lives of British royalty and officials, including three men who, in separate attempts had made attacks on the Queen's life. All three men had escaped criminal punishment by the defense of insanity. The House of Lords initiated judicial review of the case, and the 15 justices provided the following answer:

> . . . to establish a defense on the grounds of insanity, it must be clearly proved that, at the time of committing the act, the party accused was labouring under such a defect of reason, from disease of the mind, as not to know the nature and quality of the act he was doing, or if he did know it that he did not know he was doing wrong. [Glueck, 1925, pp. 178-79]

This answer, with slight modification from state to state, became the "McNaghten rule." Interestingly, the judges' answer in the McNaghten case was merely advisory opinion; there have been few instances in which advisory opinions carry weight as precedent [Weihofen, 1956]. In addition, the opinions did not constitute particularly enlightened statements even by the standards of the time and were intended primarily as a test for those psychotics of a paranoid type.[5] Nevertheless, they form the substance of a test which has survived to this date.

The problems with *McNaghten* lie in its vague and ambiguous wording. No one can be really sure what any part of the test is supposed to mean. Most courts have assumed that to "know the nature and quality of the act" means nothing more nor less than to "know that the act is wrong," hence the wording appears merely redundant. What does it mean to know that an act is "wrong"? Does the rule mean "legally wrong" or "morally wrong"? Most American cases do not define which "wrong" they are using.

The problem became apparent in the case of *People v. Schmidt*,[6] in which the defendant, Father Schmidt, confessed to the murder of Anna Aumuller. His defense pleaded insanity, claiming that he had heard the voice of God calling on him to kill the woman as a sacrifice and an atonement. In this case, the court interpreted "wrong" as "legal wrong" and found him guilty. However, upon appeal, the New York Court of Appeals ruled that "wrong" meant "moral wrong" and that Schmidt was therefore not responsible.

While the interpretation seems reasonable in the *Schmidt* case, both interpretations are vague and restrictive, and both the courts and legal writers have been reluctant to endorse either one. Waelder suggests the problem with the "moral" interpretation:

Another offender may fancy himself under such divine order but without acoustic sensations. . . . But let us go one step further . . . [and raise the question of] a man felt he received the order to kill by a less personalized power and who acted on the command of his conscience, persuaded by what he thinks is his duty toward his ideology, his nation, his party. . . . [1952, p. 381]

For Waelder, the psychiatric distinctions between the cases are negligible. In fact, the issue of "wrong" itself does not provide an adequate definition of legal responsibility. It is certainly possible for the insane to commit criminal acts, even when it is known that the act is both legally and morally wrong. In the strict interpretation of *McNaghten*, such individuals are held responsible, even though society may prefer that they be found irresponsible by reason of insanity.

The major limitation of *McNaghten* is its restriction to the cognitive, a restriction that offers little improvement over Bracton's thirteenth-century concept. Under *McNaghten*, the psychiatrist's testimony and the jury's consideration is confined to whether the defendant knew that the act he committed was wrong. As Slovenko has suggested:

Medical madness is not *McNaghten* madness. In testifying under the rule, literally and strictly applied, a psychiatrist is out of bounds in presenting evidence of the individual's mental status or capacity to control conduct. The evidence would not be responsive to the issue. [1963, p. 398]

23

One case in point is *People v. Willard.*[7] Frank Willard, an alcoholic paranoid, was convinced that he had been appointed by President Roosevelt and California Governor Pardee to arrest evildoers. Willard had twice before been committed to mental hospitals when he was once again brought before the court. On the basis of physicians' reports proclaiming Willard both insane and "homicidal and dangerous," the judge ruled the defendant insane and ordered him recommitted. As the judge was signing the order of commitment, Willard, in an angry outrage, declared that he was not insane and started to leave the judge's chambers. A sheriff tried to intercept him, whereupon the defendant drew a pistol and fatally shot the sheriff.

Willard pleaded not guilty of the homicide on the grounds of insanity and under *McNaghten*, was judged guilty. In the words of the court:

> Although [Willard] may be laboring under partial insanity, as, for instance, suffering from some insane delusion or hallucination, still if he understands the nature and character of his action and its consequences, if he has knowledge that it is wrong and criminal and that if he does the act he will do wrong, such partial insanity or the existence of such delusion or hallucination is not sufficient to relieve him of responsibility for his criminal acts. . . .

The clear limitations of *McNaghten* resulted in widespread dissatisfaction among both legal and medical circles. As a result, three alternative tests of legal responsibility have been introduced. The first of these, the *irresistible im-*

pulse test, can be traced to the 1834 Ohio case of *State v. Thompson.*[8] The primary judicial exposition of the irresistible impulse doctrine is, however, commonly attributed to Judge Somerville's decision in the 1886 Alabama case of *Parsons v. State.*[9] It was Somerville's opinion that:

> There must be two constituent elements of legal responsibility in the commission of every crime, and no rule can be just and responsible which fails to recognize either of them: 1) capacity of intellectual discrimination; and 2) freedom of will. [If mental illness] . . . subvert the freedom of the will, and thereby destroy the power of the [defendant] to choose between the right and the wrong, although he perceive it . . . [then he would not be responsible].

The irresistible impulse test has been adapted, often in combination with *McNaghten,* to expand the scope of permissible psychiatric testimony and to rectify obvious limitations inherent when *McNaghten* is interpreted in its literal sense. The irresistible impulse test has been a far from perfect solution, however, and several serious objections have been raised to it. The major argument is that impulses are never really incapable of being resisted. This follows the policeman-at-the-elbow position, which reasons that if a policeman were at an individual's side, few, if any, impulses would not be resisted. This raises major problems, as Weihofen explained:

> . . . When we enter the area of impulses that are resisted by some people but not by others, and the psychiatrist is asked

whether an urge that Tom and Dick have often felt but always successfully resisted was "irresistible" to Harry on a given occasion, there is no accepted criteria he can employ . . . "the policeman at the elbow test" which some courts have employed for irresistible impulse would permit very few diagnoses of irresistible impulse. Cases that do come under this restricted concept would probably be so far out of touch with reality that [the persons involved] could also be said not to know the nature and quality of the act. [1956, pp. 67-68]

While it can, on one hand, be argued that most, if not all, impulses are resistible, the opposite argument has been introduced in criticism of the test:

From the psychological point of view, the impulse could not have been resistible, since the act was carried out in accordance with the impulse. It is difficult for me to conceive of an impulse which is resistible but not resisted. [Zilboorg, 1943, p. 274]

While these semantic ambiguities provide, in and of themselves, sufficient grounds to question the utility of the irresistible impulse test, an even greater concern rests in the nature of the crimes to which the rule can most often be applied. In its strict interpretation, the test applies only to criminal acts which have been committed suddenly and impulsively. In 1954 the Committee on Psychiatry and Law of the Group for the Advancement of Psychiatry concluded that both *McNaghten* and irresistible impulse tests touch only a fraction of the undeterrable mentally ill. In the same year, Judge Bazelon, in *Durham v. U.S.*,[10] concluded:

. . . the "irresistible impulse" test is . . . inadequate in that it gives no recognition to mental illness characterized by brooding and reflection and so relegates acts caused by such illness to the inadequate right-wrong test. We conclude that a broader test should be adopted.

The "broader test" proved to be the *Durham* decision. Like many contemporary legal concepts, *Durham* can be traced back to nineteenth-century precedents. Judge Doe, in his dissenting opinion of the 1866 case of *Boardman v. Woodman*,[11] expressed the opinion that it was a question of fact whether delusions are a test of insanity, and that fact was for the jury to decide. In 1869 Judge Doe's views were accepted by the full court in *State v. Pike*.[12] In 1871 Judge Ladd reintroduced the reasoning of Judge Doe in *State v. Jones*[13] :

Whether the defendant had a mental disease . . . seems as much a question of fact as whether he had a bodily disease; and whether the killing of his wife was the product of that disease was also as clearly a matter of fact as whether thirst and a quickened pulse are the product of a fever . . . to attempt to provide for the jury an absolute rule wherewith to measure the mind and determine whether it is criminally responsible or not is attempting the impossible. . . . Whenever such an attempt is made, I think it must always be attended with failure because it is an attempt to find what does not exist, namely, a rule of law wherewith to solve the question of fact.

Eighty years passed until another reported case involving the defense of insanity appeared before the New

Hampshire courts. In 1951 Judge Biggs again invoked what had subsequently become known as the "New Hampshire Rule" in the case of U.S. ex rel. *Smith v. Baldi*,[14] stating that the test of responsibility should be whether or not mental illness was the proximate cause of the crime. While relatively little attention was paid to Biggs' decision, a major controversy was to develop around Judge Bazelon's decision three years later.

The defendant, Monty Durham, had a long history of criminal behavior and psychiatric commitments when a lower court's guilty verdict brought him before the U.S. Court of Appeals for the District of Columbia Circuit. Judge Bazelon, speaking for the Court of Appeals, introduced a test almost identical with that proposed by Judge Biggs: that an accused is not criminally responsible if his unlawful act was the product of mental disease or mental defect. His suggested jury charge:

> If you . . . believe beyond a reasonable doubt that the accused was not suffering from a diseased or defective mental condition at the time he committed the criminal act charged, you may find him guilty. If you believe he was suffering from a diseased or defective mental condition when he committed the act, but believe beyond a reasonable doubt that the act was not the product of such mental abnormality, you may find him guilty. If you believe he was suffering from a diseased or defective mental condition when he committed the act, and that the act was the product of that mental disease or mental defect you may find him not guilty by reason of insanity.

The *Durham* ruling met with enthusiastic support from the legal and medical professions. *Durham* at last opened the way for realistic psychiatric testimony, allowing the psychiatrist to give any evidence that was relevant to the question of the mental state of the defendant or to the question of the relationship of that mental state to the criminal act. The *Durham* test, however, never proved to be the answer to the dilemma of criminal responsibility. Only a few states ever accepted the test and even these came to conclude that it was unacceptable. Today virtually all courts have discontinued use of *Durham*, even the court that first introduced it.

Several factors contributed to the failure of *Durham*, but two areas of semantic vulnerability should be mentioned at this point. The first is the product clause, the exemption from responsibility if the criminal act is *caused* by mental disease. It is understandable that both law and psychiatry, as well as the juries that must ultimately decide issues of responsibility, maintain a concern for the cause and motivation of criminal acts. In many instances, such as homicide occurring during the commission of robbery or kidnapping, the motives of the defendant appear obvious. Historically the courts have tended to view the defendants charged with such crimes as sane and therefore responsible for the consequences of their acts [Guttmacher, 1955]. Other crimes are more difficult to explain [Cressey, 1969], particularly those crimes in which the defendant's explanations are inconsistent with the prevailing values and expectations of the society, appear to provide gains which seem to be inconsistent with the associated risks, or are committed so ineptly as to invite eventual capture of the offender.

We need an explanation for the cause of crimes which appear to us to lack understandable motivation. The concept of mental illness *seems* to provide that explanation [Hart and Honore, 1956]. When we examine the problem carefully, however, it is not altogether clear what is really meant when we say mental disease is the *cause* of criminal behavior. Mental illness is not really analogous to a physical disease with its physical symptoms. To say that mental illness, even should its physiological processes be understood, is a cause of complex criminal behavior is a logical step that has little empirical justification.

The primary diagnosis of mental illness must be made through the defendant's own behavioral and verbal responses. What we actually do is infer a state of mental illness from the actions and responses we observe; much in the way, we infer that a person is physically well when we see him performing normally. The problem results from the fact that in the case of mental illness we consider that the behavior is caused by a state which is inferred from the behavior. The circularity results in a conceptual confusion made only more devastating by its subtlety. Phillip Roche describes the process and consequences:

> We are not describing objective facts of the "mind" and of "crime" of the accused, but describing a mental process of the triers, who separate the accused from the crime by a device which explains that although the accused did the deed, it was not he but a "mental illness" that *caused* it. In

this logic the mentally ill accused is a spectator, like a dreamer, who watches himself carry out forbidden behavior and like St. Augustine, thanks God he is not responsible for what he dreams. The pain-saving feature of this process of abstraction is evident. [1958, p. 262]

It should be recognized that no empirical support exists for the generalization that mental illness causes crime. On the contrary, it is more likely that an individual diagnosed as mentally ill will be less frequently involved in criminal behavior. Nor can it be supported that the converse is generally true: that where criminal behavior is manifest, one can usually find evidence of mental illness. Clearly one can cite instances where intense social and psychological pressures precipitated criminal behavior on the part of someone diagnosed as mentally ill, but in those instances it would be more logical to attribute the criminal act to the existing pressures rather than to the condition of mental illness.

The logic of the product clause does, however, create a serious dilemma for the testifying psychiatrist. As Macniven explains:

Even the mildest psychotic illness influences the total personality and exerts some influence upon the patient's thinking and his behavior. In considering the motives determining the conduct of an insane person who commits an offense, we cannot assess with accuracy the relative influence of abnormal and normal processes in the motivation of his conduct, and the only safe rule is to assume that his offense could not be entirely uninfluenced by his abnormal state of mind. [1961, pp. 406-407]

31

The nature of the product clause presented major problems in the implementation of *Durham*. In 1957 the U.S. Court of Appeals for the District of Columbia reconsidered the issue in *Carter v. U.S.* [15] The Court considered the dilemma at length and were able to offer only one interpretation:

> The short phrases "product of" and "causal connection" are not intended to be precise, as though they were chemical formulae. They mean that the facts concerning the disease and the facts concerning the act are such as to justify reasonably the conclusions that "But for this disease the act would not have been committed."

This clarification proved inadequate. As Davidson was forced to conclude:

> Some psychiatrists say, and many more imply, that the real test should be this: a defendant should be acquitted if it can be shown that, but for a mental disorder, he would not have done the act. The trouble with this plausible sounding formula is that no one ever does anything except as a result of his state of mind. Crime is always an abnormal act in the sense that it is not what the average person does. Hence no one could ever be convicted of crime, because no act would ever be carried out except for the defendant's mental state at the time. [1955, pp. 61]

As if the dilemma of the product clause did not present sufficient difficulty, an entirely different set of problems are created by the Court's use of the terms "mental disease" or "mental defect." The original *Durham* decision chose to define "disease" as ". . . a condition which is considered capable of either improving or deteriorating." It defined "defect" as ". . . a condition which is not capable of either improving or deteriorating, and which may be either congenital or the result of injury, or the residual effect of a physical or mental disease." While there is some hope of arriving at a consensus on the classification of a "defect," the classification of a condition as a "disease" presented endless difficulties.

There are two alternatives: mental disease may be considered a juristic concept or a psychiatric one. If we choose to consider it a juristic concept, it is semantically indistinguishable from the legal term "insanity," and the test is reduced to an illogical rule stating simply that "if the defendant is insane, then he is insane." This is clearly not what Judge Bazelon had in mind. In *Carter v. U.S.* the Court clarified this issue by equating mental illness with a medically recognized illness of the mind, thus making it explicit that the term "mental illness" was thereafter to be taken as a psychiatric concept.

Unfortunately there appears to be no agreement as to what mental problems are included in the concept of mental illness. In particular, both law and psychiatry have debated whether mental illness is confined to psychosis or whether the term extends to neuroses and personality disorders. The question is critical, since the psychotic only rarely comes before the courts on criminal charges, while virtually all criminal defendants may be considered as suffering from either a neurosis or personality disorder.

The Committee on Nomenclature and Statistics of the

American Psychiatric Association, in its *Diagnostic and Statistical Manual*, offers one interpretation in the section on definitions:

> [Personality disorders are] . . . characterized by deeply in-grained maladaptive patterns of behavior that are percep-tively different in quality from psychotic and neurotic symptoms. Generally, these are life-long patterns, often recognizable by the time of adolescence or earlier. Some-times the pattern is determined primarily by malfunction-ing of the brain, but such cases should be classified under one of the non-psychotic organic brain syndromes rather than here. [1968, pp. 41-42]

Similarly, in its discussion of neurosis, the manual makes it clear that:

> [neurosis] . . . must be distinguished from psychophy-siologic disorders, which are mediated by the autonomic nervous system; from malingering, which is done con-sciously; and from neurological lesions, which cause anatomically circumscribed symptoms. [1968, p. 40]

It would appear that, in the eyes of the American Psychiatric Association, mental disease is restricted to psychoses and psychophysiological disorders, and so the courts have generally interpreted it in this manner [Overholser, 1953]. As we shall see later, this has not al-ways been the case.

The issues raised by *Durham* clearly extend beyond the semantic problems discussed above. Before we examine these issues in detail, let us consider one remaining contemporary test of legal responsibility.

In 1955 the American Law Institute drafted a *Model Penal Code* which included a section concerning the defense of insanity.[16] The section was prepared by Professors Herbert Wechsler, Louis Schwartz, and Paul Tappan, all acknowledged experts in forensic psychiatry. In their considered judgment: "No problems in the drafting of a penal code present larger intrinsic difficulty. . ."[17] Their considered deliberations essentially produced a semantic expansion of the *McNaghten* knowledge concept and the irresistible impulse test. The test they devised reads as follows:

> (1) A person is not responsible for criminal conduct if at the time of such conduct as a result of mental disease or defect he lacks substantial capacity either to appreciate the criminality of his conduct or to conform his conduct to the requirement of law.
>
> (2) The terms "mental disease or defect" do not include an abnormality manifested only by repeated criminal or otherwise antisocial conduct. . . .[18]

Unfortunately it is not clear that the semantic alterations reflected in the *Model Penal Code* test constitute serious improvements over the test's predecessors. The problems inherent in the terms "mental disease" or "defect" remain, except that the *Model Penal Code* appears, by virtue of its second clause, to restrict the tests to psychosis and psychophysiological disorders, much as the American

Psychiatric Association has implied.[19] The term *substantial* capacity, however, invites controversy. As Sheldon Glueck has suggested:

> [the test] . . . requires that the accused lack "*substantial* capacity" either to "appreciate the criminality [wrongfulness] of his conduct or to conform" it to the "requirements of law." Alternative formulations require that these capacities be "so substantially impaired" that the accused "cannot justly be held responsible," or that he lack "substantial capacity to appreciate the criminality of his conduct." Here, too, as might be expected, the question has been asked (as indeed it has been asked in other fields of law), "How substantial is substantial?" Can we all agree that substantial means something more than slight or than just a very little? But how much more? (And, incidentally, does not the provision that the accused's capacity must have been so substantially impaired that he cannot justly be held responsible amount to a non-illuminative circular statement?) [1962, p. 22]

The term "appreciate" was selected as a substitute for "know" after long and careful deliberation. It was the hope of the authors that this new word would capture the "fundamental difference between verbal or purely intellectual knowledge and the mysterious other kind of knowledge. . . ."[20] Unfortunately the mystery is sufficient to elude most juries, who tend to view the term as synonymous for "know." An explanation of the term within the test would be helpful, but the American Law Institute does not seem to have been able to provide one.

The phrase "criminality of his conduct" brings us back to the problem underlying *People v. Schmidt,* namely, the issue of legal versus moral wrong. *McNaghten* had created controversy in leaving the word "wrong" undefined, but here we see that the test of the *Model Penal Code* has taken "wrong" in its legal and more restrictive interpretation. It is unclear how the "capacity to conform his conduct," with all the accompanying semantic ambiguities of the irresistible impulse test, could provide the protection necessary to deal with a defendant such as *Schmidt.*

At the present time, most psychiatrists and lawyers are dissatisfied with all existing tests of legal responsibility. No test has yet been devised which has pleased even a significant minority of lawyers and psychiatrists for very long.

It would appear that semantics have been able to offer us little improvement in our ability to deal with the fundamental issue that Bracton confronted seven centuries ago. Few people would disagree with the belief that there exist instances in which the imposition of legally and traditionally prescribed punishments would be inconsistent with the spirit, if not the letter, of the law. The problem of distinguishing these instances from other seemingly identical events has, however, proved far from easy. The promise of scientific psychiatry has offered a tempting solution to our dilemma, but it assumes that the problem is amenable to a scientific solution. This assumption warrants further examination.

To begin, let us look again at the actual function that the concepts of *mens rea* and diminished responsibility have filled in criminal law. A careful examination of our legal structure reveals that these concepts have not necessarily been applied to issues of intent or responsibility but, more accurately, have been used as a legal device in the mitigation of punishment. For example, responsibility is a key issue in tort or civil liability, but the legally insane are nevertheless fully responsible for their torts.[21] The reasoning behind this decision was expressed in the earliest cases and has not been expanded on or changed in later opinions. William Curran considers the justification to be four in number:

(1) Tort law, unlike criminal law, is predicated on compensating for harm done, not inflicting punishment. . . .

(2) As between the insane actor who caused the harm and his innocent victim, the tort law looks with favor on the victim. It will require that the insane person compensate the victim from his available estate rather than allow the loss to fall wholly on the victim.

(3) The imposing of liability on insane persons will encourage custodians and guardians of the insane to prevent their wards from inflicting harm on others.

(4) Were a rule of non-responsibility for the insane to be adopted, it could be used as a fraudulent defense since the absence of mental illness may be difficult to prove. [1960, p. 54]

At the same time, it is clear that *mens rea* as a justification for the mitigation of punishment has not only varied with history but has also depended in part on the nature of the offense [Sayre, 1932]. This inconsistency, combined with an increasing tendency to view the law not as a device for awarding adequate punishment for moral wrongdoing but for protecting social and public interests, has resulted in serious questioning of the legal utility of concepts tied to *mens rea* or diminished responsibility [Levitt, 1928; Goldstein and Katz, 1963].

The use of mental illness as a defense also differs from other forms of legal defense in one important respect. In the establishment of legal guilt, the judicial system has placed the burden of proof on the prosecution, whose responsibility it is to establish motive, opportunity, and other elements necessary to substantiate the facts of the case at hand. However, as Graham Hughes has suggested:

> [It is] too rarely made explicit in works on criminal law that the burden of proving *mens rea* is very infrequently a real burden on the prosecution. In practice, the individual burden is usually on the defense to come forward with some evidence which takes the accused out of the normal field of liability. And the main inquiry should thus always be into the circumstances the law will permit the accused to raise successfully as a defense and, of course, into the circumstances he should be allowed to raise. [1961, p. 230]

Thus we see that *mens rea* is functionally viewed in the law in a negative sense as the absence of those conditions or qualities which, if present, would permit responsibility, rather than as a definite state of mind or determinable cognitive element which provides proof of the presence of responsibility. In its actual application, criminal *intent* is far more complex than the law would suggest. As Philip Roche has pointed out, "psychotic people do carry out criminal actions with plan, design and studied execution" [1958, p. 87]. Yet we do recognize a need to consider the psychotic state in determining appropriate punishment. We must then recognize that "intent" means more than its legal construction implies. As Roche concludes: "In the final analysis the term *intent* actually refers to how [we] feel about the wrongdoing; it is a vehicle of description and a means of fastening guilt upon the accused." [1958, p. 86].

Considering the traditional requirements of law, the concepts of *mens rea* and diminished responsibility are handy notions to have around; they provide legal sanctions for our essentially moral impulses. They allow us to make legally acceptable distinctions between different criminal acts although such distinctions may be conceptually, scientifically, and semantically incomprehensible. On the other hand, the concepts of *mens rea* and diminished responsibility may be disregarded when it is considered best to do so, either on practical grounds or in the interest of justice. For example, in the case of torts, the decision to exercise the options possible in the name of *mens rea* or diminished responsibility is largely a matter of public policy, and such decisions often appear to transcend the normal dictates of either law or medicine. In practice, the nature of these decisions is governed most directly by the extent to which they allow us to achieve the objectives which are most consistent with our moral and human conception of justice.

It is in this light that we must consider the history and consequences of *Durham*. We have seen that a formulation conceptually identical to *Durham* served the people of New Hampshire for nearly a century. It has become clear, however, that the success of the "New Hampshire Rule" was not due so much to the scientific precision or ultimate wisdom of its construction as to the fact that its use and interpretation were consistent with the prevailing values and judgments of the population it served. The use and interpretation of the same construct in the years after *Durham* present a very different picture.

Judge David Bazelon was a spokesman for a time and place far removed from rural New Hampshire. His familiarity with and admiration for psychiatry grew during a period when psychoanalytic theory was the brightest light on the horizon of human understanding. The Second World War had ended and America was entering a period when it could at last divert its attention from the demands of military survival to the recognition and understanding of human and social needs. Psychology had earned its acceptance and demonstrated its potential during the war, both as a diagnostic tool in the classification of inductees and through the human factor research which had made ours the most efficient fighting force in history.

Judge Bazelon recognized the potential of the behavioral sciences; he saw in them an opportunity to achieve justice for a society and humane treatment for those who came before the bar. In his words:

Psychiatry and the Law

> I really cannot say it too strongly—psychiatrists have a great opportunity under a liberal rule like *Durham*, an opportunity to help reform the criminal law and also to humanize their own work and increase its relevance. It is not enough for psychiatrists to point out the obvious defects of *McNaghten*—if they then act casually or with studied lack of imagination with respect to an opportunity such as *Durham* has offered. . . .[22]

This invitation opened the door for psychiatry to play an unprecedented role in the American judicial process. Prior to the *Durham* decision less than one percent of the criminal cases tried in the U.S. District Court for the District of Columbia resulted in verdicts of not guilty by reason of insanity. By February 1961 that figure had risen to 25 percent.[23] A major obstacle of *Durham*, the requirement that the act be a result of "mental disease or defect," also had a solution; in at least one instance, a major psychiatric institution simply changed its terminology. Over a weekend, without the benefit of newly discovered medical evidence, the head of the institution transferred the diagnosis of sociopath from a character disorder to a mental disease [Weihofen, 1960, p. 5].

The new role which psychiatry assumed during the late fifties and early sixties posed several questions which require close examination. The *Durham* period was associated with a judgment on the part of many eminent forensic psychiatrists that the disposition of criminal offenders should be left in medical hands [Overholser, 1953; Guttmacher, 1955; Alexander and Staub, 1956; Weihofen, 1956;

and Roche, 1958]. The assumptions behind this judgment are that psychiatry has reached a level of sophistication that permits the scientific disposition of criminal offenders, and that by leaving such dispositions in the hands of trained experts, the quality of justice and the humane treatment of offenders will measurably improve. Both assumptions are open to question.

The view that psychiatry has risen to the level of a science has been a popular one. Members of the profession take pride in their accomplishments and have taken every step to maintain the highest possible level of service and integrity. As forensic psychiatry began to make a significant impact on the criminal law, the issue of the consistency and reliability of clinical psychiatric judgments became an important one. It was hoped that by demonstrating that qualified psychiatrists could arrive at consistent interpretations of a defendant's psychiatric status, the recognition of psychiatry as a science could be established. To this end, a series of research studies [Elkin, 1947; Ash, 1949; Mehlman, 1952; Rosenzweig, Vandenberg, Moore, and Dukay, 1961; Stoller and Geertsma, 1963] were undertaken to assess the consistency and reliability of psychiatrists' clinical judgments. After examining the results of these investigations, Drs. Stoller and Geertsma of the Department of Psychiatry at the University of California School of Medicine concluded:

There is little question that these results demonstrate how psychiatrist-experts were unable to agree as to a patient's

43

diagnosis, prognosis, psychodynamics, the causes of [the patient's] problems, the feelings [the patient] was consciously experiencing, or the feelings that were latent (unconscious). They could not agree on nonsense statements couched in dynamic-sounding terms. . . . [It is] concluded that the present findings reflect circumstances which have some generality, that art far outweighs science when experts in the field of psychiatry try to say what they have discovered in another person. . . . [1963, pp. 64-65]

The realization that psychiatry was something less than an exact science became apparent in the "battle of the experts" that tended to form around criminal proceedings in which the psychiatric status of the defendant was at issue. It appeared, to the disillusionment of countless juries, judges, and lawyers, that it was possible to support any number of opinions in a given case through expert psychiatric testimony. This state of affairs, combined with the seemingly arbitrary classification of behavior as "mental disease," prompted Wertham [1955] to reflect on the apparent "psychoauthoritarianism" of the law under *Durham*. The fact that psychiatry was committing itself to the arbitration of ethical and moral issues became a concern to both psychiatry and the general public [Leifer, 1963].

The consequences of such a rapid transfer of judicial responsibility to psychiatric disposition also require that we examine the nature of treatment afforded under *Durham*. The increased number of defendants excused by reason of insanity became a source of public concern. While the public recognized a need for more humane treatment of those charged with criminal offenses, the number of acquittals influenced by psychiatric testimony raised issues of public safety. This concern led to the passage of a 1955 law providing for automatic hospital commitment upon a verdict of not guilty by reason of insanity.[24] The code also provided for an accused's commitment on the grounds that he is unfit to stand trial.

The commitment code appears to be a reasonable and humane solution to a long-standing social problem. In practice, however, its implementation poses serious legal and human considerations. Once a defendant is committed, whether after trial or without trial, his release falls under strict judicial control. In *Overholser v. Leach*[25] it became clear that the court intended to distinguish between those committed to a mental hospital following a finding of not guilty by reason of insanity and those under civil commitment:

> The phrase "establishing his eligibility for release," as applied to the special class [those acquitted of criminal offenses by reason of insanity], means something different from having one or more psychiatrists say simply that the individual is "sane." There must be freedom from such abnormal mental conditions as would make the individual dangerous to himself or to the community in the reasonably foreseeable future.

Unlike the application of the same construct under the "New Hampshire Rule," the application of *Durham* was seen as inconsistent with prevailing beliefs and values, and in an attempt to restore a sense of justice and public safety, the community turned psychiatry into an instrument of social control. Recognizing the enormous difficulties inherent in the formulation of an acceptable legal definition of insanity, we can see that psychiatry had created for itself an insurmountable task in attempting to formulate an acceptable definition of sanity. Now, however, the consequences of failure rested not on the shoulders of the court or the public but on the psychiatrists themselves. Predictably, their judgments were to err on the conservative side.

This was not a new experience. Attempts to provide psychiatric solutions to the disposition of criminal cases can be traced back to seventeenth-century England [Biggs, 1955] and Scotland [Polsky, 1955]. While the concept of commitment or indefinite sentencing appears a logical device for assuring that those convicted under criminal law will be confined only for that period of time necessary to prepare them for successful return to the community, in practice, periods of confinement under commitment or indefinite sentencing tend to greatly exceed the duration of legally prescribed criminal sentences [Tappan, 1952]. As long as psychiatry accepts the role of legal arbitrator, it will be delegated the responsibility for protecting the public interest; and as long as psychiatrists accept the responsibility for protecting the public, the psychiatric hospital will inevitably assume the characteristics of the prison system which it is intended and assumed to replace.

In the meantime, the interests and legal rights of the offender may come under serious jeopardy. A legal system operating under the latitude offered by Bazelon's conception of *Durham* creates a climate highly conducive to what Szasz [1963, 1965] has termed "psychiatric justice." Although *Durham* was introduced with the full intent of improving the quality and administration of justice, it inadvertently opened the door to a legal climate under which a defendant may be confined indefinitely without benefit of trial or any guarantee of treatment or rehabilitation. While Szasz is frequently accused of overstating his case, this fact cannot be disregarded.

The irony of psychiatry's attempt to protect the defendant has not been forgotten either by those deeply committed to the administration of justice [American Friends Service Committee, 1971; Wexler, 1973] or by the courts. In every case in which the adjudication of criminal defendants has been replaced by a system under which the disposition of the criminal offender is delegated to "experts," the procedure has been declared in violation of constitutional rights.[25]

The elusive nature of justice has challenged mankind throughout recorded history. Our seeming inability to arrive at precise and consistent judgments about ultimate truth and perfect justice has led some to question the very existence of reality in any objective sense of the word [Laing, 1968]. Our judicial system is, nevertheless, faced daily with the task of determining these same elusive and imprecise qualities. In its search it has resorted to a reliance on the judgments of a jury composed not of experts but of the defendant's peers and neighbors. The human frailties of this complex, bewildering, inconsistent, and often frustrating body have been well established [Winick, 1961].[27] We retain our jury system, not because of its scientific precision or infallible wisdom, but because we recognize that in a human society it is that same body of peers and neighbors, fully cognizant of and not uninfluenced by the prevailing beliefs, standards, and morality of the community, that defines justice.

In our search for judicial perfection we have looked to both law and medicine for answers to human and moral dilemmas. It is easy to forget that psychiatric judgments, like laws, are neither more nor less perfect than the men who make them. As long as psychiatrists are a part of their society, they cannot divorce themselves from the same prevailing beliefs and standards that ultimately reflect upon our judicial process. In one way or another it is the community that ultimately defines justice, and experience has demonstrated that a jury of peers takes its task most seriously [Kalven, 1958; Casper, 1964; Gibbons, 1969; Snortum, 1971]. While a psychiatric defense may sometimes appear to offer a means of mitigating punishment, the public has tended to prove no more retributive than the average psychiatrist and far less than the letter of the law itself. As we have seen, however, the issue is more fundamental. In the last analysis, responsibility is a moral and legal question, and as such, will never be completely susceptible to medical solutions. Our judicial system is predicated on a rule of men, not of laws nor expert opinion. We retain that system not because of its perfection but because in the final analysis it offers the most direct and humane form of justice yet devised.

Is this to say that psychiatry has no role to play in our judicial process? On the contrary. The psychiatrist, by virtue of his training and his awareness of social values, is in a unique position to communicate to a jury important aspects of the defendant that the jury may otherwise never see. The court requires and deserves qualified psychiatric opinion in the same way that it must recognize and depend on existing legal precedent. Psychiatric testimony, like the law itself, is an aid to the court. Without legal boundaries and legal tests of insanity, the jury system can too easily be reduced to the moral judgment of the most dominant jury member. And perhaps most importantly, it is the law and the legal boundaries of psychiatric testimony that provide support to a jury which must render a "guilty" verdict. To expect a jury to make such a decision without the best available information and without the support of legal guidelines would be to impose a duty more severe than we could justly require.

Legal tests of insanity serve two major functions. They are a guide to the jury in its determination of responsibility by suggesting the parameters the jury should consider in making its determination, and they set the rules for expert testimony, thus determining the ways in which psychiatrists may testify. The construction of an effective test of legal insanity, as we have seen, is a difficult task. Too often in the past, the jury has been expected to render a just decision despite the existing test, and tests of insanity have been routinely bent to fit the reality of existing situations. While some representatives of law and of medicine have come to accept this fact, it leaves the door open to potentially dangerous consequences.

Psychiatry and the Law

The role of psychiatry is to give the jury an understanding, to the best of its ability, of the mental state of the defendant. Psychiatry has succeeded in accomplishing this within the framework of a wide range of legal criteria. In the sixteenth century, testimony was offered *amicus curiae* and tended to be respected by all concerned. It is important, however, that all concerned recognize the limits of psychiatric jurisdiction. The court must recognize that psychiatric testimony can differ, that it must have the benefit of the widest possible range of expert testimony. Most important, psychiatry must recognize that it cannot retain its effectiveness if it allows society to cast medicine in the simultaneous roles of arbitrator, healer, and jailer. In the final analysis, it is the jury who must decide if the defendant's illness is such that society, as represented by the jurors, would consider it unjust to hold the defendant responsible. While no simple semantic formula can capture the spirit of that intent, we are now seeing in recent formulations of legal insanity tests [Glueck, 1962; Greenblott, 1967] an increased awareness of the subtlety and complexity of the dilemma.

Notes

1. *Muller v. Oregon*, 208 U.S. 412 (1908).

2. An outstanding review of the *Brown* decision and the historic relationship between the Supreme Court and the social sciences is provided by Rosen [1972].

3. Quoted in Sayre (1932, pp. 985–986).

4. *Rex v. Ferrer*, 19 How. St. Tr., 886, 948 (1760).

5. See for example Isaac Ray's 1838 *Treatise on the Medical Jurisprudence of Insanity*. Cambridge: Harvard University Press, 1962. See also the English case, *Reg v. Oxford*, 9 Carrington and Payne, 525 (1840).

6. *People v. Schmidt*, 216 N.Y. 324, 110 N.E. (1915).

7. *People v. Willard*, 150 Cal. 543 (1907).

8. Wright's Ohio Rep. 617, 620. See also *Commonwealth v. Rogers*, 7 Mass. 500 (1844); *Commonwealth v. Mosler*, 4 Pa. 266 (1846).

9. *Parsons v. State*, 81 Ala. 577 (1886).

10. *Durham v. U.S.*, 214 F. 2d., 862 (D.C. Cir. 1954).

11. *Boardman v. Woodman*, 47 N.H. 120 (1866).

12. *State v. Pike*, 49 N.H. 399 (1869).

13. *State v. Jones*, 50 N.H. 369 (1871).

14. 60 U.S. ex rel. *Smith v. Baldi* (1951).

15. *Carter v. U.S.*, 232 F. 2d 608 (D.C. Cir. 1957).

16. American Law Institute, *Model Penal Code*, Tentative Draft No. 4, Article 2, Section 4.01. See also subsequent drafts which contain substantially the same verbiage.

17. *Ibid*, p. 156.

18. *Ibid*, p. 27.

19. In practice this is seldom the case. See Kuh [1963] on the nature of psychiatric testimony under the *Model Penal Code*.

20. *Model Penal Code*, Draft No. 4, p. 157.

21. Leading precedents have been *McGuire v. Almy*, 297 Mass. 323

(1937) and *Van Vooren v. Cook*, 75 N.Y.S. 2d 362 (1947). The possible exception to the legal practice of holding the insane fully responsible for their torts involves actions requiring a special intent or malice on the part of the defendant.

22. From Bazelon's *Isaac Ray Award Lecture* "Equal Justice for the Unequal," mimeographed, 1961, p. 4.

23. Statistics documented in Glueck [1962, p. 116]. The figure for 1960 was 8 percent; the first 6 months of 1961 averaged 14.2 percent.

24. District Code sec. 24–301 (1955).

25. *Overholser v. Leach*, 257 F. 2d 667 (D.C. Cir. 1958).

26. See *State v. Strasburg*, 60 Wash. 106, 110 Pac. 1020 (1910); *State v. Lange* 168 La. 958, 123 So. 639 (1929); *Sinclair v. State*, 161 Miss. 142, 132 So. 581 (1931); *Baxstrom v. Herold*, 383 U.S. 107 (1966).

27. See, for example the case of Garrett Brock Trapnell, "Return of Dr. Jekyll," *Time*, January 29, 1973, p. 20.

Chapter 3

The Nature
of
Addiction

". . .the rest is just waiting."

If we are to establish a special legal status relative to addiction or hope to establish effective therapeutic programs to respond to the issues of addiction, we must first determine the nature of addiction and be able to specify precisely how addiction differs quantitatively and/or qualitatively from other human or physiological experiences. This problem is complicated, as we have seen, by the fact that there appears to be no professional consensus on the origin, nature, dynamics, or definition of addiction or its related states. Differences in the definition of addiction and the classification of addictive substances are dramatic and often completely contradictory. A review of all commonly used definitions, however, reveals that virtually all include one or more of the elements given below.

Definitions of addiction typically require that the practice: (1) be central in the individual's life, taking "compulsive" precedence over other "normal" activities; (2) is associated with an identifiable intoxication or feelings of euphoria; (3) is associated with a tendency to increase the level of usage so that greater and greater "doses" are required; (4) is associated with a substance (drug) which, when taken into the living organism, may modify one or more of its functions; often definitions require that the substance (drug) fall into a specific classification(s), which vary from definition to definition; (5) is associated with a physical dependency such that discontinuation and/or significant reduction is associated with a characteristic and specific group of symptoms, termed an "abstinence syndrome."

It should be noted that few definitions require that all five elements be present. Some definitions draw on only one or two of the criteria, or use different wordings. The classification of drugs as "addictive" or "nonaddictive" is an area of particular debate, with relatively few classification systems regarding nicotine, caffeine, or alcohol as "addictive." Often the classification as "addictive" is restricted to analgesic (pain-relieving) substances, but some classification systems include central nervous systems (CNS) stimulants and/or depressants. Other classification systems include all substances believed to produce intoxication or feelings of euphoria.

The first three criteria, although not specifically identified as drug-related, have become closely associated with the drug phenomenon. We picture the addict as compulsively in pursuit of euphoria and requiring larger and larger doses of stimulation to maintain the same level of satisfaction. In the addict this behavior is viewed as abnormal, as a symptom of his "disease." On close examination, however, it becomes difficult to differentiate this process as observed in addicts from a seemingly identical behavior observed among race-car drivers, fighter pilots, mountain climbers, or snowmobilers. In fact, most participants in physically challenging or life-threatening sports and/or occupations report experiencing feelings of euphoria associated with success at mastering the physical demands of their activities. At the same time, success in mastering one level of speed or skill results in a need to move on to situations demanding higher speed or greater skill in order to experience the same feelings of challenge and satisfaction. While a fighter pilot is required to make decisions at speeds which are incomprehensible to most civilians, the experienced fighter pilot will view the events of his occupation as taking place in ultra-slow motion [Bach, 1963, pp. 46-49].

The dynamics of life-threatening sports and professions have been examined by Erving Goffman [1967] in a fascinating study of the motivations, methods, codes, and consequences of risk and challenge. Although the activities involved vary from industrial settings to criminal activity to bullfighting, one common element links each of these pursuits:

> Physical danger is a thin red thread connecting each of the individual's moments to all his others. A body is subject to falls, hits, poisons, cuts, shots, crushing, drowning, burning, disease, suffocation, and electrocution. A body is a piece of consequential equipment, and its owner is always putting it on the line. Of course, he can bring other capital goods into many of his moments too, but his body is the only one he can never leave behind. [1967, p. 167]

Despite the danger, despite all the human and physical costs associated with such a profession, there are men and women for whom all other concerns are secondary. For these people, life is spent in what an outside observer could well consider a compulsive pursuit of physical excellence. For these men and women, physical challenge is both an ultimate goal and a central identity. As Richard Bach, author of *Jonathan Livingston Seagull*, has said:

> Divorced from my airplane I am an ordinary man, and a useless one—a trainer without a horse, a sculptor without marble, a priest without a god. Without an airplane I am a lonely consumer of hamburgers, the fellow in line at a cash register, shopping cart laden with oranges and cereal and quarts of milk. A brown-haired fellow who is struggling against pitiless odds to master the guitar. [1963, p. 28]

Peter Garrison once attempted to explain why men put their lives and hopes into the pursuit of flight: ". . .they are in thrall to something—some element of the aviator's experience that acts upon them like a narcotic upon an addict. And addicts there are—genuine addicts, who have let marriages founder and careers pass them by. . . ." [1972, p. 38]

Why, then, can we not assume that it was this "addiction" which compelled Bach to leave his wife and six children to wander the globe in a Widgeon seaplane?[1] Nor is the "addiction" confined to pilots and sportsmen. Shortly after his troupe's fatal Detroit accident, trapeze artist Karl Wallenda was asked how he could ever again return to the high wire. His answer: "to be on the wire is life; the rest is just waiting."

But let us turn now to the role of drugs in the addictive process. There appears to be little question that the narcotic analgesics, particularly the opium derivatives, have addictive potential. Increasingly, however, we are seeing a recognition of the "addictive" potential of CNS depressants, a group which contains barbiturates, hypnotics, and alcohol. If we accept this classification, and research tends to support the claim [Zwerling and Rosenbaum, 1959; Brecher, 1972], then we must recognize that alcohol cannot realistically be differentiated from other "drugs." Similarly, CNS stimulants (amphetamines) are also coming to be recognized as potentially serious drugs of abuse.

However, the distinctions become more complex as we examine the action and consequences of other pharmaceuticals. For example, the past 20 years have witnessed the introduction of a steadily growing class of ataractic (tranquilizer) medications. Ataractic tranquilizers have a different basis of operation than that associated with the barbiturate sedatives, and ataractics do not produce stupor and coma even when very large doses are involved. However, at least eight ataractic drugs; meprobamate (miltown, Equanil), Chlordiazepoxide (Librium), ethchlorxynol (Placidyl), glutethimide (Doriden), methyprylon (Noludar), methagualone (Revonal), diazepam (Valium) and ethinamate (Valmid), as well as common paraldehyde have been found to have serious abuse potential. These depressant drugs are capable of producing the phenomena of intoxication, are associated with escalating dosage, and discontinuation is associated with specific abstinence syndromes [Lemere, 1956; Hollister, Motzenbecker and Degan, 1961; Essig, 1964; Bakewell and Wilker, 1966; Ewing and Bakewell, 1967].

The recognition of abuse potential however, is not confined to analgesics, stimulants, and depressants. Within the past ten years, both hallucinogens and inhalants have become regarded as substances of abuse [Lauria, 1968]. Similarly, reviews of drug abuse also typically include discussions of both caffeine and nicotine [Blum, 1970a, Brecher, 1972]. The list, however, does not stop here. Isbell & Chrusciel [1970], in a report prepared for the World Health Organization, presented technical data on two-hundred and fifty-three additional non-narcotic psychoactive drugs and herbs considered to have an actual or potential capacity to produce distortions in perception, thinking or judgement, and which induce drug dependence.

While the substances discussed by Isbell and Chrusciel tend not to be agents of frequent current abuse, it is appropriate that we also examine the dependence liability of household agents and patent medicines. In doing so, we find that substances as common as Vitamin A [Nutrition Committee, Canadian Paediatric Society, 1971] have also documented abuse potential, while household aspirin is considered by many experts as among the most seriously abused medications [Wenger and Einstein, 1970]. Mood changes associated with the use of oral contraceptives are well documented [Hirst, 1971], and both psychological and physiological dependence on antacids [Goodman and Gilman, 1955], diuretics [Davidson and Silverstone, 1972], and purgatives (laxatives) are common occurrences [Purgatives, 1969; Love et al., 1971; Van Rooyen and Ziady, 1972].

Nor is the phenomenon of "addiction" associated solely with use of an active drug. Research on electrical self-stimulation of the brain [Olds, 1958; Heath, 1963] has revealed that both animal and human subjects develop dependencies on the electrical stimulations which follow the criteria associated with drug addiction. More interestingly, there is ample evidence that placebos[2] (inactive drugs) can cause most, if not all, of the effects due to any active drug [Beecher, 1962; Honigfeld, 1964]. The case of a female patient reported by Vinar [1969] is typical. The patient was released from hospitalization and prescribed a variety of common tranquilizers, each resulting in the patient's report of serious side effects. Only when the available medical alternatives were exhausted was she given a placebo which was presented as a "new major tranquilizer without any side effects." Only then was the patient able to function effectively in her job. Her work then progressed so well that she was promoted to a more responsible position; with her new responsibilities she began to suffer from a variety of somatic complaints. To deal with her anxiety, she found it necessary to increase the dosage of her "medication," which in turn resulted in the exhaustion of her supply. Without the "medication" she was unable to function and was readmitted to hospital:

> It seems worthy of emphasis that this patient displayed . . . the formal traits of [drug addiction]: a tendency to increase the dose; inability to stop taking the tablets without psychiatric help; an almost compulsive desire to take the tablets; and an "abstinence syndrome" with physical symptoms when deprived of the tablets. [Vinar, 1969, p. 1,190].

The "addictive" effects of placebos do not appear to be confined simply to "mild" drugs such as tranquilizers. As early as 1954 Leslie reported substituting saline (inactive) injections for morphine in addicts, without withdrawal symptoms appearing until the saline injections were stopped.[3] In fact, the dynamics of placebo effects appear to play a major role in the reported reactions to hallucinogens and marijuana. On the basis of his investigations of LSD and other psychedelic drugs, Barber concluded that "Although variations in drug-dose may produce some variations in mood, the types of moods and emotions that will be manifested appear to be closely dependent upon the situation and the subject's set and personality." [Barber, 1970, p. 65] Similarly, after reviewing the action and effects of marijuana and other cannabis derivatives: "It appears likely that the effects are dependent not only on the grade and dose of the marijuana but also on such extra-drug variables as the situation, the subject's set (for example, his expectations and motivations for taking the drug), and the subject's personality." [Barber, 1970, p. 86]

These conclusions are consistent with the discovery by Weil, Zinberg and Nelsen [1968] that subjects must "learn" to experience the effects of marijuana, and with Becker's [1953] analysis of the factors involved in becoming euphoric or "high" with marijuana. According to Becker, to attain a "high," it is necessary for the individual to have a series of experiences in which he learns to smoke marijuana, learns its effects, and learns to enjoy the sensations he perceives. This conclusion was supported in a study by Bennett [Bennett, 1971; Edwards, 1973] in which experiences attributed to marijuana were found to correspond most closely with a subject's expectations, which, in turn, were most directly related to the subject's personality. Such findings led Andrew Weil to conclude that "to my mind, the best term for marijuana is *active placebo*—that is, a substance whose apparent effects on the mind are actually placebo effects in response to minimal physiological action." [Weil, 1972, p. 94]

Some investigators have chosen to view drug addiction in a different light. The incidences of drug use and their apparent growth and expansion are seen as fitting a pattern similar to that associated with epidemics. Indeed, we frequently hear of a "drug epidemic," and the existence of such "epidemics" can be viewed as verification of the medical basis of addiction [Bejerot, 1968, 1972]. On closer examination, however, we find this distinction to be more complicated.

In June 1962 employees of a Southern textile mill were stricken with a mysterious illness. Investigation attributed the illness to the bite of insects which were brought into the factory in a shipment of cloth that had arrived from England. Reliable reports indicated that the small insect attacks the skin, the bites leaving a wound similar to the gnat bite. In about 20 minutes the victim is stricken with severe nausea and a breaking out over the body. Within a matter of days the resulting epidemic forced closing of the factory.

In their study of the June Bug epidemic, Kerckhoff and Back [1968] provide us with one of the finest contemporary accounts of hysterical contagion. Despite the consistent and specific symptomatology (so impressive that a vast array of professional talent was mobilized to cope with the problem) and the strength of the victims' belief in the reality of "the bug," no acceptable medical explanation could be found. Finally, medical experts were forced to conclude that the outbreak was almost exclusively psychogenic in nature. Given the demands of a peak production season, the personal needs of employees, and the fact that no specific complaints could be lodged against the relatively new and progressive factory, the existence of an "epidemic" at that time and place fulfilled the repressed needs of its victims. In the authors' words:

> We must conclude . . . that although it is possible to make an abstract distinction between a pure case of hysterical

contagion and a pure physical epidemic, any empirical case is likely to have elements of both . . . the fact is that the term "epidemic" is correctly used to refer to any case in which there is an unusually rapid spread and high incidence of some form of bodily disturbance. In some of these cases the balance is undoubtedly very strong on the side of some definable external toxic element's effect on a number of persons and in others (such as our case) the balance is undoubtedly very strongly on the side of the effect of some shared source of unresolved tension. But we would not expect to find cases that are purely one or the other. [1968, p. 198]

On the nature of professional response to epidemics, the authors conclude:

. . . the manifest content of the physically transmitted medical epidemic and the case of hysterical contagion are often indistinguishable. In fact, the experts who were called into our case basically used hysterical contagion as a residual category when they could not find a toxic cause for the symptoms they observed . . . . One of the points at which the two kinds of cases may be viewed as identical is the point at which the experience of symtoms becomes labeled and a plan of action is devised and carried out. In both the medical epidemic and the case of hysterical contagion, the significant manifest element is a series of persons complaining of symptoms who come to the attention of medical authorities. In both cases it is necessary for the victim to have an experience of discomfort, to define that experience as medically relevant, and to seek medical attention (or to behave so that others will seek it for him). [1968, p. 196]

The Nature of Addiction

It is not the intent of Kerckhoff and Back, nor is it our intent, to imply that the discomfort experienced by patients is ever anything but very real and very frightening. We must, however, recognize that medical diagnoses and the distinctions between cases with seemingly apparent and identical symptomatology are often complex, subtle, and not completely susceptible to medical classification. For example, a recent study of general hospital admissions [Vaillant, Shapiro, and Schmitt, 1970] disclosed that 43 percent were motivated in part by emotional distress. While only 36 percent of these cases received psychiatric consultation, less than 30 percent could have been adequately managed, even in retrospect, without general hospitalization.

Let us now turn our attention to the physiological and biochemical basis of addiction and physical dependency. As discussed earlier, Dole and Nyswander [1967] have been instrumental in the introduction of a metabolic theory of heroin addiction which has had far-reaching implications for legal and social policy. As they conclude:

> The unexpected favorable response of addicts to a maintenance program has forced us to reexamine the psychogenic theory of addiction. Historically, this theory has been based upon study of established addicts, and not upon data obtained in the pre- or post-addicted state. The so-called addictive personality therefore could be interpreted either as a cause or a consequence of addiction. [Dole and Nyswander, 1967, p. 23]

The Nature of Addiction

While their description of addiction research is not completely accurate,[4] the point is well taken, and it was this set of circumstances that led them to *infer* a biological-addiction theory. In 1970 Vincent Dole, in a paper prepared for the *Annual Review of Biochemistry*, compiled a scholarly and impressively thorough study of the biochemistry of addiction. Into this framework he tried valiantly to ground the Dole-Nyswander addiction theory. To this end, he was less than successful. While subtle biochemical alterations have been found to be *associated* with addiction, casual relationship cannot be established. As Dole concluded:

> . . . the evidence suggests that narcotic drugs affect synaptic transmissions . . . . What is not yet known is whether these neuro-transmitters are directly involved in the initial biochemical events of drug-cell interaction, or whether they reflect changed synaptic activity in regions remote from the primary sites . . . . A basic assignment for future research is to make this distinction, since the biochemical determinants of addiction are more likely to be found in events close to the primary cellular actions of narcotic drugs than in the relatively nonspecific discharges of remote neurons. [Dole, 1970, pp. 835-36]

The spirit of this theme was captured by Arnold Mandell in his review of the work of Dole and other physiologists, delivered at the *Fourth National Conference on Methadone Treatment:*

The Nature of Addiction

> In expansive moments, we who work in this field dream that the attempts to elucidate the mechanisms of action, toxicity, tolerance and physical dependence of drugs of abuse in the brain will be as productive in the understanding of brain function as the work stimulated by the discovery of the antibiotics aided in exploring cell biology. Our fantasies include ones in which a thorough understanding of the brain's chemical mechanisms of adaptation will lead to analgesics that don't produce tolerance and withdrawal, euphoriants without analgesic action that will mitigate the fear of death in the dying patient without losing its effect from long-term use, drugs which will inhibit the expression of physical dependence without being addicting, and drugs which will alter subtle aspects of human feeling states such as rage, jealousy, boredom, ennui, and demoralization without altering the brain's biology in such a way as to make the original condition worse. We fantasy these things. We aren't there yet. [Mandell, 1972, p. 21]

In our quest for medical solutions to human problems it is easy to underestimate the subtlety, complexity, and essentially adaptive nature of the human organism.

While our understanding of psychophysiology is still limited, it is likely that the fulfillment of Mandell's fantasy is a long way off indeed. The relationship between the mind and the body is a complex one [Dunbar, 1954; Canon, 1963], and inferences about causal relationships must be made with great caution. Let us first look briefly at the effect of physiological change on emotional states.

The assumption that drugs are capable of altering the personality has obvious validity, but the extent of this rela-

66

tionship can be easily underestimated. Among the landmark studies in this area is the contribution of Schachter and Singer [1962]. Subjects recruited for this research were asked to participate in a study of the effects of vitamin supplements on vision. Volunteers were given a small "vitamin" injection which was in fact adrenalin, a basic stimulant. Some subjects were told that the vitamin had side effects: palpitations, hand tremor, and a warm and flushed face. These *are* the major consequences of adrenalin so these *informed* subjects knew what to expect. Other subjects were not told to expect side effects, while a third group was *misinformed* as to the effects to expect. The subjects were then asked to wait for about 20 minutes so that the "vitamin" could take effect. In each case the subject was asked to wait with a second subject who was in reality a confederate working with the researchers. Each time, the confederate displayed either extreme high spirits or aggressive anger. As expected, those subjects who were uninformed, and particularly those who were *misinformed* as to the symptoms to expect displayed and reported emotions consistent with those displayed by the confederate.

This experiment is considered one of the earliest verifications of the theory that an individual in a state of physiological arousal for which no explanation exists will "label" his state in terms of the situation or in terms of his expectations. The theory has subsequently been confirmed in a number of independent studies. For example, Storms and Nisbett [1970] administered placebos to insomniacs, telling one group that the pills would have a relaxing effect and a second group that the pills would cause arousal. As predicted, those who were told that the pills would keep them awake (arousal) got to sleep more quickly than they had on nights without the pill, presumably because they had labeled or "attributed" [Kelley, 1967] their inability to sleep to the pills rather than to their own emotions, and consequently were less emotional and more relaxed.

From this line of research we can see that physiological states, even of a very mild nature, can have significant effects on human functioning. It is important to recognize, however, that emotions, as such, consist of two elements: physiological arousal (often at a broad or diffuse level), and the individual's specific labeling or determination of the *meaning* of that arousal.

During the late 1960s Stuart Valins [Valins, 1970] was able to significantly expand on the work of Schachter and his associates. Valins' work drew on a simple experimental model [Valins, 1966] in which male subjects were asked to view photographs of attractive young women. The subjects were told that the only laboratory space available for this "perceptual" study contained equipment to measure heart rate and that consequently the subjects would hear their own heart beat during the time they were in the laboratory. In actuality, the subjects heard prerecorded heart-like sounds in which the beats per minute were increased slightly during the viewing of randomly selected photographs. During an "independent" interview some four to five weeks later, the subjects in the original study were found to rate as significantly more attractive, photographs of those women originally viewed during the periods of increased heart-rate feedback. The experiment was subsequently confirmed and expanded in later investigations [Davison and Valins, 1969; Valins, 1970]. This research indicates that even perceived peripheral bodily changes can serve as determinants as well as correlates of emotional behavior.

But let us now examine the opposite situation. The rapidly expanding literature on psychosomatic medicine has long since established that emotional behavior can serve as a determinant as well as a correlate of profound bodily change [Dunbar, 1959]. Perhaps the most striking example of this is the concept of Vodoo death. While Voodoo death has been accepted with fascinated skepticism by laymen and professionals alike, Walter Cannon [1942] provides us with the first authoritative study of this phenomenon. In his well-documented report, Cannon not only gives an accurate clinical description of the process but offers a sound medical explanation of the dynamics. Without the introduction of external drugs, the sheer terror and anticipation of the victim mobilizes the sympathetic-adrenal system. The heart beats faster and faster, gradually leading to a state of constant contraction and ultimately to death in systole.

The above examples are part of a well-established and rapidly expanding scientific literature which confirms what many have suspected for some time, that emotional behavior and physiological change are but two sides of the same coin. All of the phenomena we have examined—from the action of narcotic drugs to the pharmacology of ataractics, from the dynamics of membership in life-threatening professions and sports to the existence of placebo reactions, hysterical contagion, and Voodoo death—are mediated by the same psychophysiological processes. In each case the primary emotional and physiological states are tied to and mediated by the functions of the autonomic nervous system [Schanberg, Schildkraut, and Kopin, 1967; Kety, 1970].

It is the autonomic nervous system, with its sympathetic and parasympathetic divisions, that regulates the visceral activities of the body and prepares the body to meet conditions of stress and danger. While this system is physiologically and biochemically complex and only partially understood, it is called upon to perform highly complex adaptive functions. Upon the recognition of subtle and often learned danger cues, this system must mobilize the body's physiological capabilities to meet the demands of the situation appropriately. In response to either stress or bodily injury, the system plays an important part in communicating impending threat to the central nervous system. In instances of actual injury or extreme psychological or physiological stress, the system mediates sensations of pain and/or euphoria, which serve both communicational and adaptive functions. Each of the sensations mediated by the system, whether it be anxiety, pain, euphoria, or simply diffuse changes in arousal level, are also capable of inhibiting the individual from applying appropriate adaptive behavior.

It is here that the introduction of physiological change in the autonomic nervous system, whether through direct action of the system or through the use of a drug, becomes a factor in a complex set of interrelationships. As we saw above, physiological arousal must be interpreted or labeled before it can be translated into an appropriate response. Once the interpretation is made, the individual is mobilized to make the response, and for sake of survival, the response made should be an adaptive one. To appreciate the functioning of the autonomic nervous system in relation to drug use, it is appropriate to examine the operation of the system in another context.

While a great deal of attention has been devoted recently to the study of physiological aspects of addiction, less effort has been spent in the investigation of psychophysiological aspects of adaptation in life-threatening situations. We do, however, have the benefit of several particularly fine research efforts—specifically, the work involving bomber pilots [Bond, 1952; Marchbanks, 1958], sport parachutists [Epstein, 1967], and combat soldiers [Bourne, 1970]. Upon close examination, we find in these groups the operation of biological processes which are physiologically indistinguishable from those encountered in addiction.

The individuals who engage in these pursuits face major hazards. To survive it is necessary to draw on physical and emotional capabilities that would not be used in other situations. In responding to the threat inherent in each of these activities, the autonomic nervous system mobilizes the strengths and perceptual capabilities of the body and plays an important part in bringing about physiological changes which allow the individual to adapt to the demands of the situation. The fact that these changes do take place is reflected in the marked acceleration of perceptual and response patterns seen in fighter pilots and in the ability of combat soldiers and parachutists to perform precise skills under conditions which others would find unendurable.

This adaptation is, however, a sophisticated emotional and physiological process. For example, it is not simply a matter of disregarding the danger or of "getting use to it." If adaptation consisted merely of ignoring the hazard or if the systems response was only the introduction of a feeling of euphoria, (as can be the case with an inexperienced person who suddenly finds himself in an identical situation without the ability to make an appropriate response), then few men could survive under demanding conditions. On the other hand, if the adaptive process consisted only of the mobilization of massive arousal it would result simply in immobilizing anxiety or blind panic.

Adaptation to life-threatening situations consists of a gradual process in which emotional patterns, physiological functioning, and behavioral responses are brought together in a unified system which results in the carrying out of actions appropriate to the demands of the situation. In short, the individual develops a "tolerance" for the conditions of the situation and undergoes the physiological changes necessary to maintain an effective level of functioning. The psychophysiological state developed to meet situational demands then becomes the norm against which all other situations are judged.

While continued use of a drug becomes necessary in order to maintain the psychophysiological state of a body which has adapted to its presence, the carrying out of actions for which the body has been mobilized becomes necessary to maintain the psychophysiological state of a body that had adapted to a demanding situation. As Epstein has concluded:

> It has already been noted that as undirected arousal mounts, because of its special aversive quality it provides an increasingly strong incentive for the organism to seek directed action, at least up to the point where extremely high levels of arousal may paralyze action. This can account for the development of fixations in organisms faced with insoluble problems, as any action, no matter how inappropriate, is less aversive than high levels of undirected arousal. It explains why people motivated by strong anxiety are highly suggestible and easily swayed by a leader or group to action that they normally would not consider. It accounts for the development of superstition, and for the readiness of patients to develop symptoms that substitute known for unknown fears. [1967, pp. 39-40]

This compelling drive accounts for the actions of combat pilots who crashed their aircraft into the ground when they were unable to carry out their assigned missions [Bond, 1952] and for the sudden voodoo-like death of pilots who are taxed to the limit of their capabilities [Jokl and McClellan, 1971]. The process is not, however, confined to those who work and play in situations that challenge men to the limit of their endurance. As we examine the process of

The Nature of Addiction

retirement from conventional occupations, we find that as few as 4 percent of the work force retire willingly, and of those who do, the vast majority regret their decision. In numbers that cannot be accounted for by age and health alone, those who retire without an active substitute for their occupational outlets die shortly thereafter [Dunbar, 1959].

Many clinicians have a simple operational definition of a drug addict: a person who feels normal on drugs [Nyswander, 1959]. In the last analysis, this is probably as realistic a definition as any. An individual with a stable and maintained drug habit is in a state of psychophysiological balance identical in its dynamics to the state associated with a stable and maintained pattern of occupational or environmental existence. The feelings of satisfaction or euphoria associated with initial drug use have the same physiological basis as the feelings of satisfaction and euphoria associated with meeting and mastering the initial challenges of a demanding profession or sport. In each case, these feelings subside as a stabalized state develops, and it will require larger and/or different drug dosage or larger and/or different physical challenges for these sensations to reappear. On the other hand, reductions in drug dosage or physical challenge will both be associated with feelings of anxiety and unpleasantness. It was the recognition of this aspect of drug addiction that led Lindesmith [1966] to conclude that it was the unpleasantness of withdrawal rather than simply the pursuit of euphoria that motivated the addict's craving for drugs.

The discovery of physiological changes associated with

drug addiction is neither surprising nor unique. Given our current understanding of human physiology, it is unreasonable to expect that any significant emotional or physical experience will *not* be reflected in physiological change. In the case of drug tolerance, the implications of the physiological changes will vary, of course, from individual to individual and will reflect, in part, the nature of the drug and the dosage involved [Thompson and Pickens, 1970]. There is no basis for assuming, though, that the dynamics of drug tolerance are any different from the dynamics of adaptation to life-threatening sports or professions discussed above, or from the human tolerances associated with adaptation to environmental temperature [Leblanc, 1966], altitude [Darling, 1963], social isolation [Brownfield, 1965], or time-oriented work and sleep patterns [Mott, Mann, McLoughlin, and Warwick, 1965]. Difficulties are associated with the readjustment of any of these dimensions, and we have no reason to believe that the difficulties associated with drug withdrawal are any more or any less significant.

In our search for a unique and distinguishing characteristic of drug addiction, we have one last dimension to consider. Society has come to accept and understand the motives which lead a man or woman to pursue a hazardous profession or engage in a challenging sport. It is more difficult, however, to understand how a "normal" person could be motivated to use a nonmedicinal drug with established habit-forming properties and a known association with serious emotional, social, and physical consequences.

The Nature of Addiction

We have considered the possibility that such persons are compelled by a physical abnormality or medical disease and found this theory to lack physiological support. The proponents of the disease theory do, however, raise a valid issue when they point out that psychosocial theories of addiction are, at best, less than conclusive. After an extensive review of the research on drug self-administration in monkeys, Avram Goldstein pointed out that: "these addicted monkeys did not suffer from unhappy childhoods or fatherless homes, nor were they alienated by oppressive conditions of life. They are ordinary monkeys. . . ." [1972, p. 27]

While there are obvious problems involved in drawing conclusions about human motivation from primate research, the point is well taken. This may well be an appropriate time for us to reconsider our assumptions about motivation in general. In attempting to understand the motivations for drug users, we should also perhaps consider what motivates a person to use alcohol, tobacco, or caffeine. Each have well-established emotional, medical, and social consequences. What factors motivate a man to volunteer to fight an unpopular war or compel him to jump out of a flying aircraft in the name of sport? Why do people devote their lives to a religion or ideology or insist on maintaining their right to own and bear firearms?

Some drug users are undoubtedly influenced by serious social factors and psychological conditions. Some see drugs as a way of dealing with stressful conditions they are otherwise unprepared to face. Still others could be considered both medically and legally insane. This could, however, be said for members of any other group we have discussed, and of members of virtually any occupational, professional, or social group.

In the last analysis, the motivations for drug use are not unlike the motives associated with any other human activity. People do the things they do because it seems to give them pleasure or because they believe that it will be instrumental in achieving an objective they consider to be important. This can be true even when the individual fully recognizes the nature and consequences of their act. An appropriate case in point is a young woman discussed by Masserman [1955]. After an unhappy love affair, she began using benzedrine in increasing quantities until she precipitated a toxic psychosis in which she developed auditory hallucinations and delusions of sexual experiences. As a result of treatment the voices left her, but she "felt so lonesome for them" that she went back to benzedrine until the hallucinations returned.

After considering the nature, dynamics, and reasons for drug abuse, the World Health Organization Expert Committee on Drug Dependence [WHO, 1969] decided to abandon use of the term "drug addiction" and adopted in its place this concept of drug dependence:

> *Drug dependence:* A state, psychic and sometimes also physical, resulting from the interaction between a living organism and a drug, characterized by behavioral and other responses that always include a compulsion to take the drug

77

on a continuous or periodic basis in order to experience its psychic effects, and sometimes to avoid the discomfort of its absence. Tolerance may or may not be present. A person may be dependent on more than one drug.

In examining this definition you will note that the term "drug" could be replaced by any one of a number of other substances, activities, or concepts, and the implications of the definition would remain the same. In attempting to formulate a legal concept of addiction we are faced with at least as many semantic and conceptual difficulties as are involved in the formulation of a legal concept of insanity. Ultimately, we must recognize that there exist no acceptable criteria for the formulation of a medical test of legal addiction.

Despite our inability to distinguish the state of drug addiction from other human and physical experiences, drug abuse remains one of our foremost social and political issues. This stems in part from the enormous social and economic costs we have learned to associate with drug dependence and with our seeming inability to arrive at a satisfactory solution to the problem. But the issue is more basic. The use of psychoactive drugs differs from other human experiences, in that drugs are specifically devised and used as disinhibitors. While the physiological sensations and behavioral changes associated with other human experiences can be viewed as a side effect of the experience, human beings use psychoactive drugs with the *objective* of achieving physiological and behavioral change.

The pursuit of this objective has been a part of human

behavior throughout recorded history and throughout all known cultures. People use drugs to symbolically and physiologically lower barriers which normally define role demands and social responsibilities. This fact presents a special problem for the formation of social and public policy and for the administration of justice. If it is the defined social function of drugs to release man from social inhibitions, how can we then hold men responsible for the violation of social codes when that violation is associated with the use of a social drug? If people drink to lower social inhibitions, how can we hold them responsible for uninhibited behavior?

Clearly these questions are a source of considerable controversy. Society is caught between the recognition and acceptance of social disinhibition, on one hand, and the fear of its possible consequences, on the other. Those who use disinhibitors or identify with family or friends who do, are reluctant to support the enforcement of social codes that fail to consider the nature and function of these drugs. Those who do not are seriously concerned for the equal enforcement of social codes which protect their life and property. The widespread use of alcohol as a disinhibiting drug has resulted in a situation where alcohol abuse laws, particularly those which affect public safety, such as driving under the influence of alcohol, are seriously underenforced. On the other hand, youth-oriented drug laws such as those regulating marijuana are selectively overenforced out of a concern for the possible consequences of large-scale youth disinhibition.

The issues, however, go deeper, and it is here that the

concept of drug addiction parallels the concepts and controversies associated with the issue of legal insanity. Underlying both addiction and insanity is a concern with the belief that human beings are subject to a wide range of inequities, social pressures, and extenuating circumstances which should be taken into consideration in the administration of justice. Given this belief and our knowledge of the social function of drugs, it is a relatively simple conceptual step to assume that drug use is a *symptom* of the presence of inequity, social pressure, and other extenuating human conditions.

It is at this point that drug addiction becomes a controversial social and political issue. If we accept the premise that drug use is a symptom of social and human conditions, it is an equally simple conceptual leap to view drug use as the *verification* of the existence of the same conditions. Unfortunately, as we have seen, the solution is not that simple.

Notes

1. See "It's a bird! It's a Dream! It's Supergull!", *Time*, November 13, 1972, pp. 60–66.

2. Placebo [L., "I shall please"]. Inactive substance given to satisfy patient's demand for medicine or as control in research studies of "active" medication. Placebos include sugar pills, bread pills, etc. Typically, the placebo is similar in appearance and taste to the substance it replaces.

3. Reported in Honigfeld [1964]. The placebo component in narcotic drug administration has been systematically investigated only in fairly recent research. Beecher [1968], in a careful review of this research, reports that placebo effects are particularly marked in patients experiencing actual postsurgery pain. In fact, the placebo's effectiveness may increase with the level of actual pain.

4. See, for example, Robins and Murphy [1967] or Robins [1972].

Chapter 4   Civil Liberties and Individual Responsibility

"... to protect Americans in their beliefs, their thoughts, their emotions and their sensations."

—*Louis Brandeis*

In their decision in the case of *Robinson v. California*, the United States Supreme Court opened the door that Judge Bazelon had entered eight years before in his interpretation of *Durham*. Six years passed before the Court was forced to confront the possible consequences of that decision in their deliberations in *Powell v. Texas.*[1] In *Robinson* the court held that addiction was an illness and that statutes which define the *status* of addiction as a criminal offense impose a "cruel and unusual punishment" and as such are in violation of the Fourteenth Amendment. However, the Court added that even though addiction itself could not be punished as a crime, states could compel addicts to undergo treatment for this illness and impose penal sanctions for failure to comply with civil commitment procedures.

In 1966 Leroy Powell appeared before the Corporation Court of Austin, Texas and was found guilty of violating a statute which made it unlawful to be drunk in a public place. Upon appeal and trial de novo in the County Court of Travis County, Texas, the defense asserted that to punish Powell criminally would be cruel and unusual punishment, contrary to the Eighth Amendment as applied to the states under the Fourteenth Amendment, since the defendant was afflicted with the disease of chronic alcoholism[2] and his appearance in public was not of his own volition. The County Court, ruling as a matter of law that chronic alcoholism was not a defense to the charge and finding the defendant guilty, entered findings of fact that chronic alcoholism is a disease which destroys the afflicted person's willpower to resist constant, excessive consumption of alcohol, that a chronic alcoholic does not appear in public by his own volition but under a compulsion symptomatic of the disease, and that the defendant was afflicted with the disease of chronic alcoholism.

Powell appealed the lower court's finding to the United States Supreme Court and in so doing, confronted the Court with the same dilemma that characterized *Durham*. If the courts accept a special legal precedent of the *status* of addiction, must it also recognize a special legal precedent for *acts* committed in association with that status? If we are to accept this special legal precedent, how and by whom would the diagnosis of addiction be made? If the diagnosis could be made, what would be the disposition of defendants found not guilty under such a satus, and how and by whom would the disposition be carried out? These were questions which would disturb, perplex, and ultimately divide the Court.

During the three months of the spring of 1968 during which the Court deliberated the fate of *Powell,* virtually every legal, medical, and moral view of the addictions and justice administration was weighed and debated. Several members of the Court held the view that Powell was an ill man, and most agreed that punishment was an inappropriate response to his illness. However, as we have seen in our discussion of the concept of legal insanity, the question goes far beyond the judicial evaluation of Leroy Powell. Finally, in a five-to-four decision, the Court held that the lower court's conviction should be affirmed.

Powell was, in every sense, a landmark decision. For years the case was relegated to the footnotes of legal textbooks, and only now it is becoming recognized as one of the few instances in which our highest court struggled with the complexities of a relationship between law and medicine that is at the heart of our social and public policies. We will examine the opinions expressed in *Powell* in some detail, not simply because they constitute the law of the land but because they represent the considered opinion of a body of men who struggled valiantly to arrive at a legal solution to one of our most pressing human problems.

Two of the issues raised during the review of *Powell* were the inability of punishment to act as a deterrent to addictive acts and the excessive cost of enforcing laws relating to addiction. The Court made it clear that these were not appropriate considerations on which to base a constitutional decision:

> Obviously, chronic alcoholics have not been deterred from drinking to excess by the existence of criminal sanctions against public drunkenness. But all those who violate penal laws of any kind are by definition undeterred. [p. 1,267]

And concerning enforcement:

> The number of police to be assigned to enforcing these laws and the amount of time they should spend in the effort would seem . . . a question for each local community. Never, even by the wildest stretch of this Court's judicial review power, could it be thought that a State's criminal law could be struck down because the amount of time spent in enforcing it constituted, in some expert's opinion, a tremendous burden. [p. 1,271]

The real problem, as we might expect, lay in the difficulty in formulating and interpreting an acceptable definition of legal addiction. The defense argued that *Powell* was a logical extension of *Robinson*, and even the dissent argued that facts introduced in *Powell* were sufficient basis for a constitutional holding that a person may not be punished if the condition essential to constitute the defined crime is part of the pattern of the defendant's disease and is occasioned by a compulsion symptomatic of the disease. The majority disagreed:

> the difficulty with that position . . . is that it goes much too far on the basis of too little knowledge. In the first place, the record in this case is utterly inadequate to permit the sort of informed and responsible adjudication which alone can support the announcement of an important and wide-ranging new constitutional principle. . . .

> Furthermore, the inescapable fact is that there is no agreement among members of the medical profession about what it means to say that "alcoholism" is a "disease." . . . there is widespread agreement today that "alcoholism" is a "disease," for the simple reason that the medical profession has concluded that it should attempt to treat those who have drinking problems. There the agreement stops. [pp. 1,261-62]

It is here that the Court recognized the implications of *Powell* in relation to the events that followed *Durham:*

> It is one thing to say that if a man is deprived of alcohol his hands will begin to shake, he will suffer agonizing pains and ultimately he will have hallucinations; it is quite another to say that a man has a "compulsion" to take a drink, but that he also retains a certain amount of "free will" with which to resist. It is simply impossible, in the present state of our knowledge, to ascribe a useful meaning to the latter statement. This definitional confusion reflects, of course, not

merely the underdeveloped state of the psychiatric art but also the conceptual difficulties inevitably attendant upon the importation of scientific and medical models into a legal system generally predicated upon a different set of assumptions. [p. 1,264]

In rendering its decision, the Court recognized a clear distinction between the punishment of a *status* as defined in *Robinson* and the commission of an act in violation of a duly enacted and constitutionally valid law:

> . . . the present case does not fall within [the scope of *Robinson*], since appellant was convicted, not for being a chronic alcoholic, but for being in public while drunk on a particular occasion. The State of Texas thus has not sought to punish a mere status, as California did in *Robinson;* nor has it attempted to regulate appellant's behavior in the privacy of his own home. Rather, it has imposed upon appellant a criminal sanction for public behavior which may create substantial health and safety hazards, both for appellant and for members of the general public, and which offends the moral and esthetic sensibilities of a large segment of the community. This seems a far cry from convicting one for being an addict, being a chronic alcoholic, being "mentally ill, or a leper. . . ." [p. 1,267]

The parallels with *Durham* are even more apparent in the Court's concern for the implications of *Powell* for the safety and security of the general public:

> . . .it is difficult to see any limiting principle that would serve to prevent this Court from becoming, under the aegis

Civil Liberties and Individual Responsibility

of the Cruel and Unusual Punishment Clause, the ultimate arbiter of the standards of criminal responsibility, in diverse areas of the criminal law, throughout the country.

> Ultimately . . . the most troubling aspects of this case, were *Robinson* to be extended to meet it, would be the scope and content of what could only be a constitutional doctrine of criminal responsibility. . . . If Leroy Powell cannot be convicted of public intoxication, it is difficult to see how a State can convict an individual for murder, if that individual, while exhibiting normal behavior in all other respects, suffers from a "compulsion" to kill, which is an "exceedingly strong influence," but "not completely overpowering." [pp. 1,268-69]

Nor was the concern of the Court confined to the safety of the general public. Recognition of the major flaw in *Durham* is seen in the Court's realization that:

> . . . the medical profession cannot, and does not, tell us with any assurance that, even if the buildings, equipment and trained personnel were made available, it could provide anything more than slightly higher-class jails for our indigent habitual inebriates. Thus we run the grave risk that nothing will be accomplished beyond the hanging of a new sign—reading "hospital"—over one wing of the jailhouse.

> One virtue of the criminal process is, at least, that the duration of penal incarceration typically has some outside statutory limit . . . "therapeutic civil commitment" lacks this feature; one is typically committed until one is "cured." [pp. 1,265-66]

89

Civil Liberties and Individual Responsibility

In the end the Court was persuaded by a recognition of the realities which led to the demise of *Durham,* a recognition that:

> We cannot cast aside the centuries-long evolution of the collection of interlocking and overlapping concepts which the common law has utilized to assess the moral account ability of an individual for his antisocial deeds. The doctrines of actus reus, mens rea, insanity, mistake, justification, and duress have historically provided the tools for a constantly shifting adjustment of the tensions between the evolving aims of the criminal law and changing religious, moral, philosophical, and medical views of the nature of man. This process of adjustment has always been thought to be the province of the states. [p. 1,269]

The essential effect of *Powell* was to affirm the Constitutional right of a community to enact and enforce Constitutionally valid laws designed to regulate the *actions* of its residents in a manner consistent with the prevailing beliefs, attitudes, and values of that community. In doing so, the Court recognized an important distinction between the *status* of a defendant and the legal implications of his *acts.* In rendering its decision, the Court maintained that there exists no definable element in the status of addiction *per se* which justifies the categorical exemption of those allegedly afflicted from liability to the enforcement of laws which govern the actions of the community at large. While the Court acknowledges that the status of addiction *may be associated* with conditions or circumstances which could justify mitigation of punishment, expert testimony concerning the addicted status of the defendant is not, in and of itself, sufficient to substantiate the existence of such conditions or circumstances. The existence of mitigating conditions or circumstances is a matter of fact which must be determined by the community through its judicial representatives.

If *Robinson* had been extended to include criminal acts associated with the status of addiction, psychiatry would undoubtedly be once again cast, in the name of "therapeutic civil commitment," in the role of social regulator. *Powell* makes it clear that *Robinson* must be restricted to a status which by definition no longer constitutes a valid crime. It is clear, however, that even by the time *Powell* was upheld, public concern for the problem of addiction and its implications for public safety had motivated creation of a wide range of civil commitment programs which raise serious questions of substantive due process.

Both the California[3] and New York[4] programs, for example, call for commitment not only of "addicts" but of those "in imminent danger" of becoming addicted. In neither case are the terms "addict" or "imminent danger" defined with any precision. California has said that both phrases were nontechnical terms which "have commonly understood meaning,"[5] and that a repeated user of drugs "is in imminent danger—in the commonsense meaning of that phrase—of becoming emotionally *or* physically dependent on their use."[6] The fact that California considers the terms "nontechnical" is interesting, since, as we have seen, there exist no acceptable medical criteria for their legal definition. Under the vague guidelines specified in existing statutes it would be possible for entire segments of the population to be arbitrarily confined without legal recourse. While statutes typically include some maximum duration of confinement, the actual period of confinement is indefinite, since there is no limit on the number of sequential commitments that can be imposed.

A closer examination of the uses of civil commitment is clearly indicated, not only because of their questionable constitutionality but because the use of civil commitment as an instrument of social regulation may be conceptually unnecessary. Historically there have been two distinct justifications for involuntary civil commitment. We may commit an individual because he constitutes a danger to himself and is in need of care or we may commit him because his presence in the community constitutes a danger to society. Although both grounds may be present in a given case, the distinction has important legal and conceptual implications, since the legitimacy of commitment must always be established under either the benevolent powers of the first justification or the police powers of the second.

The constitutional question under the benevolent power of *parens partriae* is not whether the commitment is in the interest of the individual but whether the state has the right to make that determination. Both the structure of our government and our national ideology demand serious grounds in order to justify coercion of an individual for his own good. In the words of the *Yale Law Journal*:

> It is clear that American traditions reflect a distinct bias against benevolent coercion. The conventional morality, the

national political philosophy, and the theory of representative democracy itself are all predicated on an assumption of individual self-government. Moreover, the founders thought they were writing a social contract, and the basic principle of the social contract is that restrictions on liberty are justifiable only when necessary for the *general* welfare . . . the entire constitutional scheme reflects the Madisonian principle that the power of government must be checked and balanced because men cannot by their nature be trusted to pursue the interests of others.[7]

If benevolent coercion is legitimate at all, clearly it must be subject to limits more stringent than a concern for the welfare of the individual coerced. In the absence of other guidelines the best rule is probably to assume that the ordinarily competent citizen has a right to self-government limited only by the just claims of others. *Danger to self has never by itself been made grounds for commitment or compulsory treatment.* If it were, participants in every hazardous occupation or sport would be liable to commitment, and Charles Lindberg could have been permanently institutionalized for his intention to fly the Atlantic. Similarly, no law provides for compulsory treatment of cancer or heart disease or any other noncontagious physiological ailment. Even when the condition is at a life-threatening point, such as the immediate need of a blood transfusion to maintain life, the court has held that the right of the patient to refuse treatment may be upheld.[8] If addiction is truly a "disease," what could possibly justify its unique legal status in relation to civil commitment and compulsory treatment?

Civil Liberties and Individual Responsibility

In the words of Mr. Justice Brandeis:

The makers of our Constitution . . . sought to protect Americans in their beliefs, their thoughts, their emotions and their sensations. They conferred, as against the Government, the right to be let alone—the most comprehensive of rights and the right most valued by civilized man.[9]

In reflecting on those words 35 years later, Judge Burger concluded:

Nothing in the utterance suggests that Justice Brandeis thought an individual possessed those rights only as to *sensible* beliefs, *valid* thoughts, *reasonable* emotions, or *well-founded* sensations. I suggest he intended to include a great many foolish, unreasonable and even absurd ideas which do not conform, such as refusing medical treatment even at great risk.[10]

Obviously even Justice Brandeis would recognize *some* point at which legal intervention is justified, but we cannot overestimate the seriousness of civil commitment, either to our democratic tradition or to the lives of the individuals involved. The constitutional case law on civil commitment has provided little in the way of precedent, which is understandable in view of the difficulties inherent in attempting to deal with the issues involved at other than an individual case level. Official commitment decisions have been left for the most part to the ad hoc discretion of institution officials and the local courts. While this allows the decisions to re-

94

flect the unique features of each case, as well as prevailing public concern, appropriate legal safeguards must be assured [Ennis, 1971].

In the absence of other extraordinary circumstances, the essential requirement needed to justify involuntary, benevolent civil commitment cannot rest simply with the apparent actions or stated objectives of the individual involved. Behaviors must be examined in terms of the individual's capacity to accurately assess the implications of the behavior in question. In short, the individual must be unable to accurately evaluate the existence and consequences of relevant alternative. Obviously some "addicts" lack this ability, but there is *no* legal or medical support for the assumption that "addiction" *per se* justifies that conclusion.

As we examine the language of the civil commitment sections of *Robinson* and the local and national statutes pertaining to the involuntary, civil commitment of addicts, it becomes clear that the authors are actually referring to civil commitment under police power. The distinction is a critical one, because if an addict is committed on the grounds that he constitutes a danger to the community, it is irrelevant that he may personally benefit from treatment, just as it is irrelevant to the requirements for imprisonment of a suspected criminal that he may receive treatment in jail. Involuntary civil commitment under these terms and in the absence of established violation of a duly enacted and constitutionally valid law constitutes, in effect, preventive detention. While some officials maintain that this procedure is

95

more humane and has less of a social stigma associated with it, it is difficult to see how being labeled a "dangerous addict" is less damaging than being labeled a criminal. Aside from the legal procedures invoked, the distinction in the deprivation of liberty and conditions of confinement may be no greater than the "hanging of a new sign—reading 'hospital'—over one wing of the jailhouse."

The only legal precedents which can be offered for such large-scale implementation of civil preventive detention draws on the well-established right of the state to quarantine the potentially contagious[11] and confine tuberculars.[12] The extension might be appropriate if we could establish similarities between the medical dynamics of the transmission of tuberculosis and increases in the rate of addiction. Unfortunately no such relationship can be established. While it is true that "addicts" often attempt to introduce friends and acquaintances to drug use, the participation of the "victim" is qualitatively and quantitatively different from that associated with the contraction of tuberculosis. The involuntary civil commitment of addicts is in reality more analogous to the indefinte confinement of those suffering from the "June Bug epidemic" than to the treatment of tuberculars. We have no greater assurance of its practical success, and the constitutional and human consequences of its application are no less severe.

This does not mean, however, that we are powerless to deal with those who proselytize the use of drugs. A law making proselyting a criminal offense would be as constitutionally valid as laws prohibiting solicitation and could be enforced through the conventional judicial process.

Civil Liberties and Individual Responsibility

It is conceivable that there are circumstances in which the police power application of civil commitment is the only remaining method of maintaining public safety. However, the power of the state to confine solely on the grounds of probable dangerousness to others must be subject to limits at least as stringent as those that govern the confinement of actual criminals. In particular, the state must sustain as heavy a burden of proof in order to detain a dangerous person as it must to imprison a criminal; that is, dangerousness must be demonstrated beyond a reasonable doubt.

Obviously some "addicts" constitute such a danger by virtue of psychiatric disability, but typically these cases fall appropriately under the jurisdiction of benevolent civil commitment. Other addicts constitute a clear danger to the community by virtue of established criminal acts, but, as we have discussed, there is nothing inherent in the status of addiction which exempts these individuals from traditional legal prosecution. To subject the remainder of a population, which is poorly defined at best, to liability for involuntary civil commitment is both inconsistent with our constitutional tradition and unsupported by the available medical and legal evidence [Kolb, 1925b; Joint Committee, 1961; Brecher, 1972]. The only justification for proposing such a drastic step is the belief that our traditional legal and governmental structure is incapable of responding to a social problem that is seen as threatening the safety and security of the nation.[13] This conclusion would be, to say the least, premature.

Civil commitment is an unfortunate but necessary exception to our national policy of individual self-government. Properly applied, it represents an imperfect but acceptable compromise between the rights of the individual and the rights of society. Improperly applied, it provides a way of doing thoroughly what the criminal law cannot do at all: depriving a citizen of personal liberty without due process of law.[14] The state cannot combine an inadequate police power justification and an inappropriate exercise of benevolent paternalism into a jointly sufficient basis for involuntary civil commitment.

Notes

1. *Powell v. Texas*, 392 U.S. 514 (1968).

2. Alcoholism can most appropriately be viewed as a drug addiction in which the drug of choice is alcohol.

3. California Welfare and Institutions Code, secs. 3000–09, 3050–54, 3100–10, 3150–53, 3200–01, 3300–05 (West 1966).

4. New York Mental Hygiene Law, secs. 200–12, *as amended*.

5. In *In re* De La O, 59 Cal. 2d 128 (1963).

6. In *People v. Victor*, 62 Cal. 2d 280 (1965).

7. Civil Commitment of Narcotics Addicts [1967, pp. 1168–69].

8. See, for example, *In re* Estate of Brooks, 32 Ill. 2d 361 (1965).

9. In *Olmstead v. United States*, 277 U.S. 438 (1928).

10. In *Application of President and Directors of Georgetown College*, 331 F. 2d 1000, 1016–17 (D.C. Cir. 1964).

11. *Compagnie Française de Navigation à Vapeur v. La. Board of Health*, 186 U.S. 380 (1902).

12. *Moore v. Draper*, 57 So. 2d 648 (Fla. Sup. Ct. 1952).

13. In *Korematsu v. United States*, 323 U.S. 214 (1944), concerning the exclusion of citizens of Japanese ancestry from their homes during World War II, the Court made it clear that "[n]othing short of apprehension by the proper military authorities of the gravest imminent danger to the public safety can constitutionally justify either [exclusion from homes or permanent night-time curfews] . . . Compulsory exclusion of large groups of citizens from their homes, except under circumstances of direct emergency and peril is inconsistent with our basic governmental institutions."

14. Existing civil commitment laws would require commitment of an addict even if he had not committed a crime and medical testimony indicated that he could not be helped by treatment. This may well be interpreted as inflicting cruel and unusual punishment for the status of addiction. See, for example, *Rouse v. Cameron*, 373 F. 2d 451 (D.C. Cir. 1966).

Chapter 5

Systems of Social Regulation

". . . every right implies a responsibility; every opportunity, an obligation; every possession, a duty."

—*John D. Rockefeller, Jr.*

Although drug addiction is seen as a major contemporary social issue, the rate of addiction actually reached its highest level in this country during the late nineteenth century. Far less was known about narcotics at that time, but patent medicine manufacturers did recognize that adding a little opium or morphine to their products did a lot to improve sales. At the the same time, general practitioners discovered that opium and morphine had an astonishing ability to "cure" almost any illness. By the turn of the century, over 600 patent drugs containing opiates were available on the open market [Towns, 1912], most omitting the actual nature of their contents from the label.

During this period the use of prescription or over-the-counter medications containing opium derivatives was a common practice for virtually any ailment that one would use an analgesic or tranquilizer for today. This included everything from anemia and insanity to headaches and "women's trouble." Morphine was even recommended as a substitute for alcohol, and the practice of physicians converting alcoholics to morphine did not completely end until the 1940s [O'Donnell, 1969]. Proper gentlemen who would never consider using alcohol because of religious or social objections found narcotics both practical and convenient. As we might expect, nineteenth-century opium users were similar to contemporary users of alcohol, tranquilizers, and patent medicines: middle-class, middle-age, and more often than not, female.

At the turn of the century the public and professional attitude toward opium began to change, and slowly narcotics became recognized as a danger and a vice. The medical profession came to consider narcotics a danger not only because they were habit-forming but because the pain-relieving characteristic of narcotic drugs serves to mask actual symptoms and makes responsible medical practice difficult or impossible. The public, on the other hand, saw the use of narcotics as an expensive and immoral habit and wanted to avoid passing that habit on to future generations.

The first step toward the control of opiate addiction came in the form of passage of the first Pure Food and Drug Act in 1906.

The 1906 Act required that medicines containing opiates and certain other drugs must specify their contents on the label. At the same time, drug traffic had become a matter of worldwide concern, a concern that culminated in passage of the 1914 Harrison Narcotic Act.[1] The Harrison Act was motivated in part by international political considerations,[2] but also out of the same public concern that resulted in the control of thalidomide and hexachlorophene—a belief in legitimate, legislative responsibility to public health and safety. The intent of the Harrison Act was simply to make narcotic drug traffic a matter of legal record and to limit the production and sale of opiates to medical and scientific endeavors.

The ultimate intent of the Pure Food and Drug Act and the Harrison Narcotic Act was to reduce public liability to the hazards of narcotic addiction. To this end, the legislation can be considered a success. The rate of opiate addiction has declined from an estimated level of 1 in 400 at the turn of the century to approximately 1 in 1,200 at the present time, and opiate addiction among the populations originally involved is all but nonexistent.[3] The original program of legislative control and citizen education was supported by the vast majority of the population, and a recognition of narcotic hazards has led to a major change in the drug-use patterns of the general public.[4]

While the public became increasingly aware of the dangers of opiate use, it also recognized that significant numbers of men and women were deeply involved with their drug habit. For the most part, these were respectable middle-class citizens with long-established histories of using opiate-containing medicine. Most users were well aware of the habit-forming potential of narcotics, supported legislation to prevent the spread of addiction to the young, and had no desire to become involved with underworld suppliers. Addicts applied to boards of health for relief, and the public sympathized with their dilemma. At the suggestion of U. S. Treasury Department agents, approximately 44 clinics, or dispensaries, were established in various cities for the sole purpose of dispensing drugs to addicts in order to prevent their exploitation by illegal drug peddlers [AMA, 1966].

The creation of these "maintenance" clinics seemed a logical and humane solution to a serious problem that grew out of technological change and social progress. By today's standards, an addict supporting a 50-dollar-a-day habit through black-market sources could purchase his supply through a clinic for the price of a pack of cigarettes. Drugs supplied through clinics offered quality and price control, were free of underworld influence, and greatly simplified the drug-control responsibilities of law-enforcement agencies.

Despite the fact that many of the clinics were poorly organized, badly operated, and politically sensitive, the idea was good. There is little doubt that the maintenance clinics could have been operated successfully in a way that would have allowed the original generation of opiate users to live out their lives in comparative comfort while still protecting future generations from unwitting exposure to narcotics. This was the plan the public envisioned and supported. It was not the way things turned out. Much to the horror of the general public, it was discovered that not everyone wanted to be protected against the dangers of drug abuse.

In retrospect it is difficult to distinguish fact from fiction in examining the events that followed the opening of maintenance centers during the 1920s. It is clear that most centers did operate with the best of intentions and that older addicts appreciated and respected their existence. But there were abuses; it was not so much the fact of abuse alone as the nature of the abuse that alarmed and outraged the public. From the passage of the first narcotics control legislation to the present time, the public has witnessed a shift in narcotic drug abuse, from middle-class adults who considered opiates as "medication," to an entirely new phenomenon of deliberate drug abuse among the young, the poor, and the disadvantaged.

In 1920 Britain passed its own Dangerous Drugs Act, which served the same function as the Harrison Act in the United States. Despite the fact that Britain had a negligible addiction problem at that time, in 1926 a system of maintenance was also established [Mahon, 1971]. When the first report of the Interdepartmental Committee on Drug Addiction (First Brain Report) was issued in 1958, Britain seemed pleased with the results. In 1958 there were only 442 known addicts in Great Britain. By 1964, the publication date of the Second Brain Report, the situation had changed: "There has been a disturbing rise in the incidence of addiction to heroin and cocaine, especially among young people. . . . There should be powers of compulsory detention of addicts. . . ." [Great Britain, 1967, p. 13]

In their 1965 study of drug use in Britain, Brill and Larimore [1968] noticed striking similarities between the "new" British addict and the American "street addicts." While the British addiction problem had been almost completely confined to individuals addicted in association with medical treatment, like our early American addicts, Britain now had a new addiction phenomenon:

> The youth and gregarious nature of the new type addict has led to an active spread from person to person . . . [they are] . . . "beatnik" types, unwilling to work, often quite unkempt in appearance, untrustworthy, unreliable, amoral, manipulative, and difficult, but not physically aggressive. [1968, p. 9]

Great Britain is a very different country from the United States, both politically and socially. Addiction had never been a major problem in Britain, and it took several decades longer for the British experience to evolve. But the dynamics are very much the same [Ausubel, 1966]. Every attempt to supply illegal drugs through a legal distribution system has resulted in the same pattern of abuse and the same shift in the nature and character of the abuser: programs designed to treat the needs of one generation become a platform for the initiation of subsequent generations.

Americans find this incomprehensible. Drug laws are designed to protect citizens from inadvertent exposure to a known danger. It is one thing to understand the needs of an aging addict and help him avoid criminal contacts that come from supporting his unfortunate habit, but it is quite another to contribute to the addiction of youngsters. By and large, Americans respect the law. Why would anyone want to violate a law that was designed to protect them? And, of all Americans, the public sees its *greatest* responsibility to the young, the poor, and the disadvantaged. Whey should these people, in particular, choose to engage in such obviously deviant behavior?

Logical reasoning tells us that there can be only two possible explanations: they are criminals or they are diseased. If we assume that those who knowingly abuse drugs are criminals, and we can find evidence to that effect if we try, then it is logical to enact strict enforcement measures to deal with them, the logic being:

It should be possible to stamp out the drug problem. Admittedly, it would take martial law to accomplish. Every avenue of importation must be blocked. Armed guards can be placed around every medical supply, and physicians can be given police protection. The black-market prices will admittedly skyrocket, and measures must be taken to guarantee the loyalty of those entrusted to the security effort. Civil liberties will, of course, have to be suspended.

107

Systems of Social Regulation

This approach is obviously extreme and one we are not yet prepared to use. There is, after all, an alternative—we can simply do nothing:

> Drug laws obviously don't deter everyone, but then there are few laws that do. By keeping drugs illegal we at least can't be accused of condoning drug use. If those who choose to become involved with drugs have to buy their supplies at exorbitant black-market prices, that's their problem—after all, they asked for it. If they turn to crime to support their habit, it's the job of the police to stop them.

This is a plausible line of reasoning, which obviously accounts for the present state of our national drug policy. However, when someone points out the "alarming" crime rate and suggests that we all may be murdered in our beds just to support some addicts' habits, then people tend to be receptive to alternatives. The public becomes particularly receptive to alternatives when it sees its teen-age sons smoking marijuana or finds it daughters arrested in a drug raid:

> These people are obviously sick. No one in their right mind would use those drugs. If they weren't hooked by some pusher, then they must have been under some unendurable psychological or social pressure. Look at their environments, something had to go wrong somewhere. Besides, most of them really want to stop anyway, but they just can't. The pusher is their only source and crime is the only way they can support their habit.

So we try taking drugs out of the hands of criminals and setting up a legal system of drug distribution. The logic is defendable; according to it, addiction is a "disease," so we give the "patient" the required "medication." The logic also tends to satisfy the public's concern for safety:

> . . . until we understand our society better—until we determine why drugs are wanted in the first place and then remove those causes—heroin should be provided to those who need it by hospitals, clinics, and doctors under government regulation. This may not cure addiction, but it greatly enhances our ability to control the distribution of heroin. It will cut down the enormous profit now reaped by the underworld, and it will cut down the crime committed by addicts. . . . [Rector, 1972, p. 242]

The problem is that it just doesn't seem to work that smoothly. While the number of "addicts" should remain stable or be reduced through attrition, the number seems to grow, particularly among the young. Reported abuse of the system is frequent; while it is difficult to tell how valid each particular charge is, it is usually possible to document enough instances of abuse to give the public second thoughts. Ultimately the public begins to consider that it is being exploited and that the system designed to treat one group is actually initiating another. When those involved with abuses of the system are found to also be involved in other criminal or anti-social activity, proponents of the criminal theory of addiction have that much more to support their argument.

Systems of Social Regulation

Both the general public and the professions involved become embroiled in a controversy, caught in the dilemma of supporting a solution that may be interpreted as condoning a crime while adopting a solution that can be interpreted as punishing the sick. More energy, professional effort, and literature are spent in attempting to resolve this controversy than in dealing with any other aspect of the drug problem. Proponents of each position cite the need for greater research, but the lack of conclusive research findings is cited by everyone as support for their position. The debate rages: *Is addiction a crime or disease?*

No amount of research will ever resolve this controversy. As we have seen, addiction may be *associated* with crime or illness or both. Nowhere, however, in all of the available medical and legal evidence is there anything with which to establish that *addiction* is either a crime *or* a disease. The only accurate generalization that can be made is that drug use is a behavior and addiction is a status. All other assumptions rest on the interpretation of the parties involved.

It has become a truism to say that there are as many reasons for using drugs as there are drug users. It is important, however, that we examine some of those reasons, if only to appreciate the role interpretations play in the dynamics of drug abuse. The real question, however, is not why people use drugs but why people chose to use *illicit* drugs. As we have seen, drug use is a nearly universal phenomenon. The incomprehensible fact that puzzles administrators, policy-makers, and the public is why one portion of the population refuses to make their drug habits conform to current social policy. Let us briefly examine some of the possible explanations.

Convenience

Some illicit drugs, particularly marijuana, are considered cheaper, cleaner, and less prone to side effects than other "social" drugs. Alcohol, it is reasoned, is associated with hangovers and violent behavior; marijuana is not. This position is not only consistent with popular belief but is even supported by reputable experts [Grinspoon, 1971]. Some members of the community simply weigh the probability of apprehension, which in some settings is realistically slight, against what they consider to be the benefits, and conclude that the risk is justifiable. Obviously not everyone that has ever used marijuana has submitted the decision to such rational analysis, but many undoubtedly have.

Magical Belief

The media is a frequent target for criticism by those concerned about current drug issues [Fort, 1969; GAP,

1971]. Most common are references to the youth-oriented media, which point out that as many as 40 percent of the popular songs at any given time have drug themes and that the advertising of over-the-counter medicines implies that drugs are the solution to all human problems. The dynamics, however, are far more subtle. Advertisements tell children that if they eat a particular breakfast cereal they will become big and strong, and parents also encourage children to eat by pointing out the special beneficial qualities of particular foods. While many critics imply that the media may have some sinister motive for representing drugs in a particular light, children have always been taught that some substances and/or objects have special "magical" qualities.

Adults do not necessarily intend to imply that particular objects or substances have magical qualities, but in the eyes of a child all things that cannot be understood are magic. The rites of the church, particular ceremonies, patterns of diet and dress—are all seen by the child as having a relationship to particular outcomes and, as such, are believed to have special properties. During adolescence these beliefs are transferred to particular patterns of dress, speech, and behavior which are almost completely ritualistic.

John Whiting [1959], in a fascinating cross-cultural study of the dynamics of childhood, has demonstrated the power and subtlety of this phenomenon. The desire to believe in magic of some type is not confined to childhood, however. Superstition and ritual are seen as central in the lives of boxers and bullfighters [Goffman, 1967], combat soldiers [Bourne, 1970], and in the very assumptions of organized religion. Milbourne Christopher [1970] demonstrates that religion need not assume a traditional form; the same powerful beliefs and customs can be seen clearly in the followers of seers and psychics.

Dependence on a drug can and often does serve the same function as a good-luck charm, a religious medal, or a hefty weapon. People carry each of these in the belief that they supply strength and courage and that these objects have a special power which goes beyond their physical properties. A drug, however, has a property which few other objects of superstition can claim. If you assume that an object has special qualities, what could be better than being able to consume that object and both literally and symbolically make it a part of you?

Drugs, in part because of their ingestable nature, have played an important part in religion throughout history[5] [LaBarre, 1964; Graubard, 1967; Brecher, 1972]. Drugs used in religious experiences have always been closely guarded secrets, kept from the congregation and reserved for the chosen few. The forbidden status of illicit drugs provides the same hidden fascination. While much of our understanding of the operation of superstition and ritual comes from primitive societies, we must remember that youth itself is a kind of primitive society. Behavior we can only interpret in terms of deviance or defect can have a rational logic when viewed from that perspective.

The function that our media does perform is to specify the behavior that each forbidden drug is assumed to produce. As we saw above, emotional behavior must consist of two components: physiological change and an interpretation of the meaning of that change. Except in extraordinary circumstances, a drug will provide only physiological change;[6] the user must provide the label or interpretation. The mass media, combined with street lore and the expectations of the user, provide the basis for interpreting the change produced by a given drug, and tell the user how he "should" respond in a given drug setting [Sharoff, 1969; Linsky, 1970].

Surmountable Challenge

. . . the ex-addicts who speak in schools and at civic meetings, it is true, do not portray the cure as easy. They describe it as requiring a heroic effort of will and the ability to endure grave hardships—like climbing a mountain, or like crossing a desert. Young people, of course, are attracted to precisely such challenges. [Brecher, 1972, pp. 82-83]

During the sixties, it was common to see students at high schools or colleges walking between classes or sitting under a tree with a copy of *Synanon*. The book had all the drama and romance of a best-selling novel—a villain (drugs), a hero (a "reformed addict"), a challenge (the "cure"), and a happy ending (addicts win the battle against drugs and live together happily ever after). Together, the heroes build a life in the face of overwhelming odds (and parental disapproval) and dedicate their lives to saving other fallen souls.[7] Conquering drugs has all the drama and fascination of climbing Everest or shooting the rapids of the Colorado, and you can do it all in the comfort of your own living room.

Reality Testing

Richard Blum and his associates [1970b, 1972b] have become the chief spokesmen for a view that sees illicit drug use as a response to permissiveness. On the basis of his extensive research, Blum concludes that permissive, affluent home environments, combined with a liberal school setting and sensationalization of drug use, are associated with drug supplies and what is considered a safe setting for their use. Blum believes that this permissiveness on the part of parents and school officials is a "camouflage for irresponsibility."

Blum maintains that illicit drug use appears to be *less* among lower-income minority families than among well-off white families. Also, according to Blum's research, but contrary to popular belief, many parents are well aware of their children's drug use and condone it. While drug abuse may be more prevalent among the middle class, it is clear that drug abuse affects all social and economic groups, and at least one aspect may be shared in common by all adolescents who use illicit drugs.

Parents, as well as school officials and others who serve to provide a parental function, are faced with a dilemma: they must constantly work to achieve a balance between an environment that is so restrictive that it prevents a child from growing and an environment that offers so little structure and security that it constitutes a threat to the child who must live in that environment. The task is a difficult one, but achieving a solution to it is essential to the security of the child [Rousell and Edwards, 1971; Edwards, 1973]. Adolescents, as well as everyone else obliged to live amid social interdependencies, must know the limits they are allowed to function in and feel secure that those they depend upon will care enough to provide safe and nondestructive boundaries.

Drug abuse is a topic which parents and society as a whole feel strongly about. An adolescent who uses illicit drugs and allows his parents to "accidentally" find out may be testing parental respect and concern. When a society maintains, on one hand, that narcotic drugs constitute a hazard and, on the other, condones the use of narcotics by members of that society whom they supposedly care about, then we have reason to question its sincerity. When a social or racial group maintains that the drugs they use are distributed with the willing consent of the government in an attempt to deliberately subvert that same social or racial group, then we must closely examine the meaning of that statement.

Tactical Use

As we have discussed, the meaning of drug use is nothing more nor less than the meaning we provide in our interpretation. Drug abuse is, however, one of the few things that will usually guarantee a rapid and heated interpretation. As such, it takes on overtones other behavior lacks and acquires a tactical value other alternatives may not possess.

The late Saul Alinsky, a man widely respected as a teacher of radical tactics, once lectured at a very conservative college. Afterward, some of the students came to his room to explain their problem:

> Their problem was that they couldn't have any fun on campus. They weren't permitted to dance or smoke or have a can of beer. I had been talking about the strategy of effecting change in a society and they wanted to know what tactics they could use to change their situation. I reminded them that a tactic is doing what you can with what you got. "Now, what have you got?" I asked. "What do they permit you to do?" "Practically nothing," they said, "except—you know—we can chew gum." I said, "Fine. Gum becomes the weapon. You get two or three hundred students to get two packs of gum each, which is quite a wad. Then you . . . drop it on the campus walks. This will cause absolute chaos. Why, with five hundred wads of gum I could paralyze Chicago, stop all the traffic in the Loop." They looked at me as though I was some kind of nut. But about two weeks later I got an ecstatic letter saying, "It worked! Now we can do just about anything so long as we don't chew gum." [1971, pp. 145-46]

Symbolic Meaning

All social acts are subject to literal as well as symbolic interpretation. To share a drink with a friend or co-worker may be interpreted as a gesture of friendship, as an indication that normal role constraints or formalities may be temporarily suspended or as a sign of the existence of sufficient trust to allow one person to become disinhibited and consequently somewhat vulnerable in the presence of another. Indeed anthropologists argue that these symbolic functions are of critical importance in explaining the social function of alcohol.[8] These same symbolic functions take on a new dimension when they involve the use of an illicit drug. All of the original meaning is retained, but by sharing an illicit activity, an actual and symbolic level of mutual trust is implied. By becoming accomplices in the same illegal act, a level of comaraderie is established which would otherwise be impossible in the context of a social situation.

Participation in illegal activity has played a social role throughout history in everything from childhood pranks to college initiation ceremonies. Obviously not all illegal activities are singled out for this special function. For an illegal act to have symbolic meaning it must be distinguishable from crimes motivated purely out of personal gain; therefore crimes which either have no victim or an easily rationalized victim who is not unduly exploited serve this purpose particularly well. When the activity offers some intrinsic pleasure to the participants and at the same time requires violation of an unpopular or infrequently enforced law, it becomes especially attractive. Obviously both prohibition and many of our current drug laws fit this description [Kaplan, 1970]

Illicit drug use provides other symbolic functions, depending on a particular social context. Armand Mauss [1969] has attempted to determine why such a flagrant and heavily penalized form of deviance as marijuana use occurred so extensively among upper-middle-class students. His research indicates that male high school students consider marijuana use a part of college life and that use of marijuana in high school is a symbolic preparation for college. Illicit drug use also functions as a symbolic act in the conflict of generations [Feuer, 1969; Lipset, 1970] and can be seen as a "rite of passage" into adulthood [Van Gennep, 1960].

Each social group assigns its own meaning to a particular act, and since drug use is subject to an extraordinarily wide range of interpretations, predicting its symbolic meaning in a particular context is difficult enough to make generalizations impossible [Wilkins, 1965; Whitehouse, 1969]. In some cultures drug use is seen as an appropriate and adaptive form of behavior [Sutter, 1969]. For others, it becomes a way of dealing with entire sets of complex feelings, attitudes, and roles, as well as interpreting and defining them in terms of a single behavior, or in Epstein's words, "symptoms that substitute known for unknown fears."

Erikson [1957], in a classic study of social adaptation, analyzes this phenomenon in a way that provides a vital clue to the dynamics of the "June Bug" epidemic and an insight into the basic dynamics of deviant behavior in all of its forms. As Erikson observed: "In the absence of clear-cut organic symptoms, a real illness which can't be helped is the most precious commodity . . . patients have in their bargaining with society for a stable . . . role." By singling out drug addiction, mental illness, juvenile delinquency, or any other "social disease" for special attention and treatment, we may dramatically shape the form and prevalence of the social problems which we as a society must ultimately confront.

Disease Correlate

We cannot discount the fact that some drug users are mentally and/or physically ill. In some instances drug use can and does contribute to both physical and mental ill health. At the same time, mental or physical illness can make the use of drugs appear to be an attractive alternative. It is important to recognize, though, that rarely does one *cause* the other. In fact, like the relationship between crime and mental illness, it is difficult to establish that drug use and illness even occur together with more than random probability [Dole and Nyswander, 1967].

Regardless of the motivation or combination of motivations which contribute to initial illicit drug use, and regardless of how conscious or unconscious those motivations may be, the illicit drug user soon finds himself in a unique and deviate subculture.[9] As with social movements [Toch, 1965], the same factors which serve to bring people together in a behavior that is not shared by the remainder of the community also serve to separate and isolate them from the larger society. In most instances this feeling of isolation provides a powerful motivation to recruit new members into the subculture.[10] This fact is reflected in the findings of the Joint Committee of the American Bar Association and the American Medical Association on Narcotic Drugs:

> Deliberate proselyting by drug peddlers in order to expand their market plays only a minor role in spreading addiction; rather, addiction spreads from person to person. Initial doses are usually supplied to the neophyte by a friend, as a friendly gesture. [1961, p. 170]

In addition to a desire to expand their subculture, illicit drug users must attempt to find some way of bringing their beliefs, attitudes, and behavior into correspondence [Fishbein, 1966]. Most drug users, at least initially, share most of the beliefs and values of the society-at-large. Since society maintains the position that illicit drug use is, by definition, improper, then drug users must either stop using illicit drugs or change their beliefs and values. If they elect to continue their illicit drug behavior, it is necessary to

121

develop a set of rationalizations [Hartung, 1969; Edwards, 1972] which allow them to justify that behavior. Their options are four in number:

1. *Denial of the problem* argues that drug use and experimentation is not an issue of consequence to the general public. It makes a distinction between "mild" drugs which are safe and "hard" drugs which an enlightened user will avoid. It further maintains that drug use will have little or no effect upon participants, that the decision to use drugs is a matter of individual conscience, and that what one person chooses to put into his or her body should not be subject to public debate or control.

2. *Denial of responsibility* points to a multiplicity of environmental factors, from the War and social unrest,[11] the pressures of day-to-day existence, and the deterioration of the American family, to the rapid change, the loss of old values, and social and economic injustice. It blames the mass media and commercial advertising for popularizing and advocating drugs and escape, and points to the "pusher" and peer group pressure as seducing unwilling victims to a fate they could neither anticipate nor control.

3. *Denial of the accuser* offers variations of the above and points accusingly at those who condemn drug use yet tolerate alcohol abuse and medicine cabinets filled with "prescriptions" for mood drugs, diet pills, pep pills, and other chemical escapes. It says, "You don't object to drugs; you object to *our* drugs and *our* life styles." It cites the Vietnam War, hypocrisy, and injustice as additional reasons why the

"establishment" is not qualified to question the morality of an emerging generation.

4. *Appeal to higher loyalty* transcends all of the above. It maintains that the existing social order is so thoroughly corrupt and destined to collapse that it must no longer be taken seriously. It equates the drug experience with religious phenomena and elects the "priests" of the new order. It transforms law and morality, turns inward, and shuts the door to outside intrusion.

The impact of drug use depends, of course, on the extent and nature of use, as well as the number and function of other activities in the user's life. The occasional marijuana user whose drug use is confined to social settings in which marijuana is accepted and who otherwise functions as a member of the larger community, will be less affected by his role as an illicit drug user than the person whose life is built around illicit drugs. As a person becomes more deeply involved in drug use, however, he or she is increasingly subject to both the physical consequences of the drug[12] and the social and psychological impact of membership in a deviate group.

As a person becomes a part of any group that is isolated from the mainstream of society, it becomes increasingly difficult for him to judge reality. The outside is viewed with increased suspicion and symptoms of paranoia become evident. Members of a deviate group become susceptible to influence by other group members, and the identity and self-concept of both the group and its individual members becomes increasingly diffuse and unstable. This is a situation prone to a wide range of psychogenic phenomena [Toch, 1965]. Not only is the situation conducive to hysterical contagion, it becomes a classic setting for other forms of group and individual disturbance. In 1877 Lasegue and Falret identified and described a process which they termed *folie a deux* and which Gralnick[13] defines as "the transference of delusional ideas and/or abnormal behavior from one person to one or more others, related or unrelated, who have been in close association with the primarily affected person." This process provides a very viable explanation of the patterns of psychopathology observed in groups such as the Manson "family" and offers a particularly appropriate basis for evaluating what often is assumed to be a causal relationship between illicit drug use and mental illness.

Members of deviate groups are also susceptible to the larger society's interpretation of their actions. Just as people must interpret and label physiological changes, they must also interpret their own behavior. The reasons that may influence a person to initially engage in a particular activity are not necessarily those that influence continuation of these same activities [Allport, 1937]. The explanations a society offers for the actions of its deviate members become critical factors in an individual's interpretation of his own deviance, and the explanations can serve to create powerful self-fulfilling prophecies for the individuals involved [Goffman, 1963; Walster, Aronson, and Brown, 1966; Zimbardo, 1967; Houts, 1970]. In most instances, particularly when identities are ill defined and unstable, people tend to become what others expect them to be.

This fact has critical implications for our interaction with those we chose to call "addicts." If we choose too quickly to focus on the deviance or irresponsibility of a particular individual or insist on making unjustified generalizations, we can force people into roles they may not otherwise assume [Rock, 1968; Scheff, 1968]. If we treat a person as an irresponsible child, it can only increase the probability that he will act like one. On the other hand, our actions can also serve to support his basic rationalizations.

If we treat drug addicts like criminals we do so at the expense of reinforcing any existing paranoia or Robin Hood delusions that may already exist. By the same token, if we treat addicts as though they were "sick," they will soon learn to exploit the secondary gains associated with the sick role [Erikson, 1957; Butler, 1970]. In either case, the power to punish the "criminal" or compensate the "victim" of illness rests with the larger society. Whatever action society takes must therefore be interpreted as part of interaction between a powerful actor (society) and a less powerful actor (the "addict"). These situations of differential, or *asymmetric*, power have presented unique problems in the formation of public policy throughout history [Mauss, 1954; Schwartz, 1967; Thibaut and Gruder, 1969; Titmuss, 1971].

As a rule, people do not like to accept gifts they cannot return or to be subject to the control of a person or group having powers they cannot match [Homans, 1950; Thibaut and Kelley, 1959; Schopler and Bateson, 1965; Kelley,

1968]. In responding to such situations each party will respond not only to the behavior and actions of the other but also to the motives we *attribute* to those behaviors and actions [Adams, 1965; Berscheid and Walster, 1967; Blau, 1967; Schopler and Thompson, 1968].

If we assume that addicts are criminals and concentrate our attention on their crimes, then addicts will not only see themselves as criminals but will see their criminal behavior as being proportional to our concern. If we then suggest providing free drugs to addicts as a way of decreasing their crime, the addict must assume that his threat to society is very great. This perception of great power allows the addict to believe that his powers are as great as those of society and allows him to resolve the seeming inequity that originally characterized the relationship. He can then reason that "our power is as great as theirs; the only reason they offer us free drugs is because they are afraid of us; well they can't get off that easily." Obviously this is not necessarily society's **real** motivation, but the addict can only respond to the interpretation that seems most reasonable to him. Unfortunately his response can be an increased criminal involvement, which can only result in a verification of the criminal stereotype.

On the other hand, if we adopt the position that addicts are the victim of a disease and offer to provide free "treatment," then this response is also subject to interpretation. The likely reactions are twofold. First, this approach reinforces the "addict's" belief that he is a victim of circumstances which are beyond his control and supplies the addict with the basis for assuming that he occupies a special status with a special entitlement. Since society has not been known for its generosity in the past, any steps it is now taking are probably inadequate and exploitive, and this justifies any retaliation the addict may elect to inflict [Moynihan, 1969]. Second, this approach puts the control of drugs in the hands of society, making the addict dependent on society for his supply. The easiest way to resolve this dependency is to subvert the distribution system and channel as many drugs as possible out of the hands of society and into a distribution system controlled by addicts. This, of course, involves the initiation of new users, which, by virtue of the special status addiction has assumed, will find drug use even more attractive then ever.

It is to this complex and shifting set of dynamics that our national drug policy must be geared. In view of the difficulties inherent in any policy approach, it is understandable that we have not yet formulated a perfect solution to the drug issue. This is further complicated by the fact that problems with any one approach usually result in its replacement by a different and possibly contradictory strategy, which, in turn, is abandoned when it fails to provide a solution. Even if any of the popular policy approaches were workable, the fact that none has been applied with consistency may account for their failure. Let us, then, examine briefly the probable result of each of these policy positions.

The strict enforcement approach is a viable alternative in situations where the society is threatened by a clear, present, and identifiable danger which society uniformly opposes. Evidence of this can be seen in our enforcement of kidnapping laws and in the Herculean accomplishment of the U. S. Public Health Service in containing major epidemics. Unfortunately, few drugs laws meet these criteria. Drug violations consist, in virtually every instance, of a transaction between a willing seller and a willing buyer. But even if enforcement could intercept every illicit drug shipment, this could not eliminate drug abuse. Anyone with the intelligence and resources to bake a cake using a recipe can manufacture psychoactive drugs [Abood, 1970; Brecher, 1972]. To control drugs through enforcement would require confiscation of every substance from prescription drugs to banana peels and placebos that is considered capable of producing physical or psychogenic dependency.

The problem goes far beyond logistic considerations. To focus on the control of a substance is to equate drug abuse to St. Augustine's dreams; it implies that man is not responsible for his actions. The responsibility for drug abuse rests ultimately with the user. To perpetuate the myth that drugs are responsible for their abuse is like perpetuating the belief that guns are responsible for shooting people. Neither are more than thin rationalizations which can never exempt human beings from their responsibility for the events they set in motion. Systems of social regulation that rely on the control of substances and objects are poor public policy and ultimately contrary to the interests of the people they serve.

The major alternative to the enforcement approach lies

in the development of an American "British System." Proponents of this alternative [Schur, 1963; Lindesmith, 1965; Zinberg and Robertson, 1972] maintain that addiction is a medical problem and that the responsibility for dealing with the problem should be left in medical hands. The idea is not a new one, of course, and the Harrison Act never implied that this would not be possible.

The scope of medical practice under the Harrison Act relied on judicial interpretation. From 1915 to 1925 five major cases involving a physician's use of narcotic drugs came before the Supreme Court. The first case to interpret the Harrison Act was *United States v. Jin Fuey Moy*,[14] in 1915, in which the Court ruled that an addict's physician was his only legal source of drugs and that possession of illegally gotten drugs was a violation of the Harrison Act. *Webb v. United States*,[15] in 1919, was even more restrictive in deciding that it was illegal to prescribe drugs for an addict while not attempting to cure his addiction. Another *Jin Fuey Moy*[16] case, in 1920, strengthened *Webb* by stating that a physician could not "cater to the appetite or satisfy the craving of one addicted to the use of the drug." Finally, in 1922 the Court ruled, in *United States v. Behrman*[17] that prescriptions for addicts were illegal regardless of the purpose, even if it was to cure or withdraw the addicted person.

In each case an increasingly restrictive interpretation was influenced by flagrant abuses by the physicians involved, and the Court conceded that the decisions had to be taken in that context. In 1925, however, the Court reversed its earlier position in its review of the case of Dr. Charles O. Linder. Dr. Linder had been convicted of providing four tablets of drugs to a woman undergoing withdrawal. In its review the Court stated that *Harrison* was a revenue measure and that it:

> . . . says nothing of "addicts" and does not undertake to prescribe methods for their treatment. They are diseased and proper subjects for such treatment. . . . What constitutes bona fide medical practice must be determined upon consideration of evidence and attending circumstances.[18]

It is clear, then, that as early as 1925, in *Linder*, the United States Supreme Court recognized the disease concept of addiction which was to be viewed as a precedent when it appeared in *Robinson*. It further left the treatment of addiction to the physician within the bounds of "fair medical standards." This was followed, in 1935 and 1938, by the construction of federal narcotics hospitals in Lexington, Kentucky and Fort Worth, Texas. The definition of these facilities as "hospitals" further indicates a governmental recognition of addiction as an illness. The Court also made it clear, in its four earlier decisions, that there exists a point when "treatment" becomes support of the addiction, and that the distinction must be left to the dictates of bona fide medical practice and fair medical standards.

In the evaluation of the British drug program, Zinberg and Robertson explain the events that led up to the Second Brain Report as resulting:

... primarily out of the medical profession's own reluctance to deal with addicts. Indeed, the Brain Committee found that the [physician] overprescribers "had embarked on the treatment of addicts out of a sense of duty because they felt that the treatment facilities elsewhere were inadequate." Addicts did not make good patients. They were often unruly, clamored for higher doses, and were difficult to cure. Many doctors believed that their disease was the result of weakness, and for that reason felt more concerned about the organic maladies of other patients. The medical profession, in short, was prejudiced against addicts, and few doctors would treat addicts at all. [1972, p. 126]

We find, then, that it is not the medical profession of Great Britain that provides treatment to addicts but a small minority of physicians who do so out of a personal "sense of duty." The situation in America does not appear to be really that much different. While the proponents of the "British System" maintain that American physicians are reluctant to treat addicts under *Linder* because the Federal Bureau of Narcotics has fostered the punishment view of addiction, this explanation is really not consistent with the way the medical profession sees its own responsibilities. American physicians have never found their treatment options under *Harrison* and *Linder* to be unduly restrictive.[19] In the words of the American Medical Association:

It is the physician's responsibility to relieve pain by eliminating its cause if possible . . . continued administration of drugs for the maintenance of dependence is not of itself a bona fide attempt at cure, nor is it ethical treatment. . . . [AMA, 1970, pp. 83-84]

While addiction may be considered a "disease" in the broad sense of the term, it is by no means *just* a medical problem.[20] The rationale for the British System is based on two assumptions, that drug use has health implications which fall under the legitimate jurisdiction of the medical profession and that the responsibility for the control of drugs should be delegated to the medical profession. If you follow these two assumptions to their logical conclusion, then liquor licenses would be granted only to physicians and gun control would be delegated to gunsmiths. As we have seen with civil commitment, you cannot combine two inadequate justifications into a jointly sufficient rationale for an otherwise unacceptable course of action.

A distinction must be made between drug use as a part of medical treatment and the use of drugs for recreation or to support an addiction. The medical profession as a whole and the public as a whole appear to agree on where that distinction must be drawn. Attempts to create an American "British System" are motivated by a strong desire to find some solution to the problems that confront drug addicts. Unfortunately this is not the solution; the medical profession neither seeks, nor is especially qualified, to act in the role of drug mediator.[21] Most physicians view their primary responsibility as the treatment of illness, and the maintenance of addiction is seen as inconsistent with the demands implied by the responsibility.

It is clear, however, that there are exceptions. Physicians use and dispense drugs in a manner consistent with their own medical and *moral* judgment [Polenz and Feder, 1968; Greenblatt and Shader, 1971; Brecher, 1972; Blum and Associates, 1972a]. In the absence of other guidelines, delegation of discretionary responsibility for drug control to the medical profession or to any other single profession is a commitment to the most liberal moral interpretation of any member of that profession. To adopt such a position would be to disregard everything history has taught us about legal medicine and public policy.

We have said that the rights of the individual must be limited only by the just claims of others. The formulation of effective public policy rests in the attempt to achieve a social order in which the rights of both the community and the individual receive maximum protection. Policy decisions are by definition choices between imperfect solutions. As long as individuals engage in activities that violate the prevailing morality of the community, we will have both social and legal issues that can never be fully resolved. It is critical, however, that we refrain from invoking poorly formulated or blatantly unconstitutional policies in the name of expedience.

Each of the legal, medical, and social approaches to the issue of drug abuse which we have reviewed contain basic conceptual flaws that would ultimately undermine their effectiveness. Drug abuse is an emotion-laden topic; it is understandable that the public and the professions alike would grasp at any solution that seemed to offer hope of meeting the problems inherent in the drug issue. In our eagerness to meet a genuine and critical challenge, we have attempted to make policemen out of physicians, psychiatrists out of the courts, censors out of the media,[22] and propagandists out of our educational and law-enforcement institutions.[23] Not only have these attempts failed to meet the needs of the community, they have failed to provide realistic and responsible help and support to the individuals most directly affected by drug abuse.

Ironically the opposing factions and theorists are not as divided in their objectives as their public positions may cause them to appear to be. Most agree that there are realistic and significant dangers in some forms of drug use, both legal and illegal. Most agree that these dangers are of legitimate public concern and that issues of public safety appropriately fall within the scope of our legal and public health institutions. Most feel that addicts are as entitled to the constitutional protection of the law as any other citizen and that his or her legitimate medical needs should be met as competently and professionally as those of any other citizen. Most will ultimately recognize that drug abuse is a social issue and that the community not only has the legal right and responsibility to respond to that issue to the best of its ability, but that attempts to impose solutions contrary to the prevailing judgments and beliefs of the community are doomed to failure.

Responsible public policy must be founded on the assumption that the individual members of the community it serves can and will, unless it is established to the contrary, conduct their activities responsibly and accept the consequences of their actions. There is no basis in law, medicine, or public policy to categorically exempt drug users from this assumption. In responding to each of its responsibilities, and in particular in responding to the issues of drug abuse, our social institutions are expected to function with the same wisdom and judgment we expect from a responsible parent. For many young people, their first encounter with judicial or medical institutions involves drug abuse. It is our responsibility to assure that these encounters represent the highest possible level of fairness, responsiveness, and professional service.

Everyone must recognize, however, that those who use drugs, whether legally or illegally, *are* subject to the just claims of others. These claims include full recognition of and compliance with the duly enacted and constitutionally valid laws designed to protect the safety and property of other community members. It has always been a rule of law that ignorance or mistake of the law never excuses a person.[24] This, too, is founded on public policy and applies to drug users as surely as it does to other members of the community. An individual's status of addiction has no legal bearing on his responsibilities under law; being under the influence of a drug or drugs is not a legal defense unless it negates some element of the offense.[25]

It is also possible, under constitutional interpretation, for a community to enact laws that relate specifically to the abuse of drugs. For example, it is understandable that a community may wish to prohibit persons from appearing in public while under the influence of drugs. It is also reasonable for a community to prohibit by law the sale of drugs or the solicitation of drugs when drugs are provided without charge. Laws regulating advertising have been established in the past and can be established within the bounds of constitutionality.[26] Laws regulating the abuse of drugs —for example, "driving under the influence," which regulates public acts—are also constitutional and extend to all forms of drug use. It is also possible to consider being under the influence of a drug while committing a criminal or negligent act as a circumstance of aggravation and impose specific penalties for this independent of the crime or negligence.[27] In particular, administering a drug to another person without that person's knowledge has the potential of producing serious or fatal consequences. Such an act would justify the harshest legal sanctions.

None of the legal alternatives discussed above is intended to regulate or have the consequences of regulating the private acts of individual citizens. In each case the alternatives are designed simply to protect the just claims of other community members. There are, however, other special considerations involved in drug use, and the clearest medical and legal precedents can be found in aviation medicine [Cutting, 1962]. For example, one medical complication associated with high-altitude flight is a condition known as hypoxia, which results from an inadequate supply of oxygen. The consequences of hypoxia are similar to the symptoms of drug use—euphoria, unjustified feelings of confidence, slowing of reflex response, diminished cognitive capability, and ultimately unconsciousness. After due deliberation the Federal Aviation Administration passed a regulation[28] which prohibits pilots and crew members from flight above specified altitudes without the use of supplemental oxygen. Under this regulation, a pilot must use oxygen even if he is the only one in the aircraft and even if the aircraft is not over persons or property.

In a sense this was an unprecedented move in aviation, since pilots have always been permitted by law to fly even homemade aircraft over isolated areas despite the hazards involved. It was reasoned, however, that the use of experimental aircraft is a hazard the pilot can and must evaluate, and the consequences of failure are borne entirely by the pilot involved. Hypoxia, on the other hand, presents a different problem. The consequences of hypoxia are such that the capacities of those affected are reduced sufficiently to render impossible the realistic evaluation of both the situation and the condition. This law, then, is not an attempt to restrict the right of the individual to engage in clearly evaluated but nevertheless hazardous activity but a regulation designed to protect society from the consequences of a medical condition with symptoms that makes evaluation of the hazards impossible.

Aviation also provides a clear precedent for the restriction of rights on the basis of drug use. The status of addiction does have clear implications for the capability of a person to perform specific occupational duties; performance of flight duties can be restricted, by law, on the basis of drug use, ranging from heroin to sodium bicarbonate.[29]

137

Systems of Social Regulation

Addiction is a status and as such should not be a basis for discrimination in employment or civil rights. It should be recognized, however, that conditions relating to the status of addiction can and will have a bearing on the ability to perform specific tasks. It is therefore justifiable to restrict persons from particular occupations, not on the basis of status but on performance capability.

Society is still left with a need and responsibility to respond to the problems of those citizens who have adapted to the use of illicit drugs and perhaps also a desire to make available for limited recreational use drugs currently prohibited by law. The two concepts are difficult to distinguish; for the purposes of public policy, they may be indistinguishable. There are no perfect solutions to this problem. Society will always face a point when in good conscience it must refuse to endorse particular forms of drug abuse. At the same time, it does have some available alternatives to current practice which retain both the community control essential to any workable policy and the medical support this problem demands. Here again, aviation medicine provides an analogy that can help put the issue in perspective.

Flight personnel, like members of many other occupations or sports, are required by law to meet certain physical requirements. It is the responsibility of the Aviation Medical Examiner to investigate the health of flight personnel and certify that they meet these requirements. His responsibility is to both the individual and the society that depends on the safe performance of that individual. He certifies only the medical status of the individual.

138

Our society currently permits the use of specific drugs and maintains relatively little control over their use and distribution. This control is the legal right and responsibility of the community; attempts to remove control from the community can only fail. For example, the community licenses the number and operation of establishments which sell alcohol and cigarettes and regulates cigarette and liquor advertising. The State of New Hampshire prohibits the advertising of liquor and restricts liquor sales to state-operated facilities which resemble post offices in their unobtrusive appearance.[30]

At the same time, we see an increasing tendency toward liberalization of drug control in both public opinion and the law itself. For example, *People v. Sinclair*[31] established the right of a state to exercise supervisory powers over marijuana violations and declared that marijuana had been erroneously classified as a "hard narcotic." As the community revises it statutory policy toward drugs, it is clear that a revision of its distribution policies will also be in order.

It is both feasible and constitutional for the community to establish state-operated drugstores for the purpose of regulating the sale of psychoactive drugs and substances. The community can require medical authorization for each sale, and that authorization can be restricted to a particular drug in a particular quantity. The responsibility of the authorizing physician would be restricted to certification of the fact that the drug and dosage involved will not be detrimental to the health of the individual, and the authorizing physician will be held responsible for the health and

139

safety of the user in the same way physicians are held responsible for the individuals they certify for occupational and athletic purposes.

The dispensing facility would assure cost and quality control and operate under the supervision of a community board. This board could review all drug distribution; final authorization for distribution of any drug would rest with the board. The board would insure that all distribution is by medical authorization and could further require that each user meet specific legal requirements, demonstrate an understanding of the true medical consequences of the drug and dose involved, and demonstrate an understanding of and liability to the laws that govern drug use and community membership. The system could, of course, be extended to drugs currently distributed through other legal channels.

The one characteristic that has traditionally distinguished successful social groups is the formation of an active and visible consumer population which is both willing and able to represent and regulate the actions of its members and to distribute and bear responsibility for the costs of its actions. Drug users, in part because of their unique legal, political, and social status, have never been required or able to develop this capability. Consequently drug use remains a poorly regulated, deviate activity which attracts and perpetuates social irresponsibility.

It is a well-established principle of democratic government that the users of a service bear the cost and responsibility which that service entails.[32] There is no medical or legal basis for assuming that drug use should be an exception. A public policy of providing free drugs to "drug addicts" on the basis of their status is analogous to providing publicly supported airlifts to "addicted" skydivers or maintaining wars for the benefit of old soldiers. All are equally irresponsible and are supported by the same level of medical, social, and legal evidence.

The cost of whatever programs we adopt in response to the drug issue must be borne by the participants in the programs. This includes the cost of the drugs involved, as well as the costs of administration and enforcement and the cost of treatment and rehabilitation of those who require it. This condition is dictated not only by sound public policy and the interest of society but, as we shall see, by the interests of the individual participants as well.

Notes

1. Harrison Act, 38 Stat. 785 (1914) as amended in 26 U.S.C.

2. In this case, legal responsibilities associated with United States governing of the Philippine Islands and fulfillment of obligations under the International Opium Conference of 1911 and 1912. Opium, of course, has a long economic and political history. See, for example, Owen [1968].

3. Figures based on the computations of Terry and Pellens, quoted in Kramer [1970].

4. In a nation that consumes two billion gallons of alcohol and fills 180 million prescriptions for psychoactive drugs per year, it is clear that we are talking about a *change* in drug-use patterns, not a *decrease* in drug use.

5. We see a similar dynamic in the use of bread and wine in religious services.

6. Most normal individuals, without pain, find the simple physiological effect of drugs (particularly opiates) to be unpleasant at best. See, for example, Lasagna, von Felsinger and Beecher [1955] or Chein *et al*. [1964].

7. For a poignant and surprisingly well balanced account of such a quest, see Sheehy [1971].

8. This view has been expressed by Sherwin Feinhandler.

9. Deviance can, of course, serve a social and psychodynamic function. See, for example, Ackerman [1971] for an introduction to the literature on family homeostasis.

10. The exception to this rule consists of physician drug addicts [Winick, 1961] and others who must maintain their deviate roles in relative isolation.

11. The Vietnam War is easily overestimated as a factor in introducing Americans to narcotics. While approximately 4½ percent

142

of our servicemen took advantage of low-cost opiates in Southeast Asia, the majority of addicted veterans began their drug use outside the service. See, for example, Patch, Raynes and Fisch *Vietnam Heroin Addicts in Boston* (unpub., undated manuscript.) Psychoactive drugs and tranquilizers play only a minor role in combat medicine. As with most hazardous occupations, drug use is not an asset in combat [Bourne, 1970]. See also Robins [1973].

12. Physical consequences are well documented and will not be reviewed in this report. In addition to psychiatric symptoms, typical consequences include renal, cardiac, and respiratory complications. One recent source [Brecher, 1972] implies that the toxic effects of illicit drugs are overestimated, but physical consequences must also include indirect complications such as hepatitis, malnutrition, nervous exhaustion, and serious accidents associated with drug use.

13. A review is provided in Waltzer [1963].

14. *United States v. Jin Fuey Moy*, 241 U.S. 394 (1915).

15. *Webb v. United States*, 249 U.S. 96 (1919).

16. *Jin Fuey Moy v. United States*, 254 U.S. 189 (1920).

17. *United States v. Behrman*, 258 U.S. 280 (1922).

18. *Linder v. United States*, 268 U.S. 5 (1925).

19. Legal precedent does not appear to play that great a role in determining medical policy. The medical profession has been adamant in its stand on emergency treatment despite the fact that legal action has never in history been taken against a physician as a result of having provided emergency care [Chayet, 1969].

20. The federal court went an additional step in clarifying *Linder* in its 1934 decision in the case of *Strader v. United States* 72 F. 2d 589 (10th Cir. 1934). The interpretation is consistent with AMA policy in that it " . . . forbids the giving of a prescription to an addict or habitual user of narcotics, not in the course of professional treatment, but for the purpose of providing him with a sufficient quantity to keep him comfortable by maintaining his customary use. Neither the statute nor the regulations preclude a physician from giving an addict a moderate amount of drugs in order to relieve a condition incident to addiction (withdrawal distress), if the physician acts in good faith and in accord with fair medical standards."

Systems of Social Regulation

21. The medical profession has been troubled by "script doctors" since the passage of the Harrison Act [AMA, 1966; Brecher, 1972]. The Group for the Advancement of Psychiatry has advised that "Although it may embarrass the physician when he cannot clearly define a disease, he should not prescribe medications as a way of handling his own anxiety as well as the patient's distress" [GAP, 1971, p. 25]. At the same time, the House of Delegates of the American Medical Association has urged that steps be taken to emphasize the particular vulnerability of physicians to drug dependence [AMA, 1970].

22. Some spokesmen [Fort, 1969] see the media as the prime perpetuator of drug abuse. Often, however, suggested methods for regulating the media constitute clear violation of First Amendment rights.

23. Drug education has proven to be an overwhelming failure (see, for example, *Behavior Today*, 1972, *3*(46), p. 2; or the *Journal of the Addiction Research Foundation*, 1972, *1*(6), p. 1). In most instances, drug education programs have failed to observe even the elementary principles of attitude change [Hovland *et al.*, 1953; Zimbardo and Ebbesen, 1969].

24. See *State v. Brown*, 38 Kan. 390 (1888) for a discussion of the distinction between ignorance of *law* and ignorance of fact. See also *Model Penal Code*, Proposed Official Draft, sec. 2.04.

25. See *Model Penal Code*, Proposed Official Draft, sec. 2.08. Being under the influence may be taken into consideration in determining malice aforethought. *State v. Hudson*, 85 Ariz. 77 (1958). Being under the influence may be also cited to establish absence of intent. See, for example, *People v. Walker*, 38 Mich. 156 (1878). However, when recklessness establishes an element of the offense, being under the influence does not constitute a defense. The use of drugs to "nerve" oneself to commit a crime already decided upon renders the lack of intent due to being under the influence invalid as a defense *(State v. Robinson*, 20 W.Va. 713 (1882).

26. See, for example, the Cigarette Labeling and Advertising Act, 15 U.S.C.A., secs. 1331–40 (1972).

27. This has been urged by Coke and Blackstone but never adopted

[Perkins, 1972, pp. 537–38]. The analogy would be laws making unpremeditated homicide committed in the course of a premeditated crime a premeditated homicide; or laws which make use of a firearm in the commission of a crime, a crime in and of itself. See also, Wechsler and Michael (1937).

28. Federal Aviation Regulation 91.32, Amendment 75, June 17, 1970.

29. See Cutting [1962, pp. 31, 62]..

30. Alcoholic Beverages Law, N.H. Rev. Stat. Ann., chaps. 175–82 (1964), as amended.

31. *People v. Sinclair*, 387 Mich. 91 (1972).

32. The sole exceptions to this principle are social welfare programs which are operated on the basis of their benefit to the community as a whole and not the "right" of the direct beneficiaries to receive particular benefits. These programs must be distinguished from workmen's compensation or insurance programs in which participants distribute shared risk and assume associated costs. This does not, of course, preclude the right of social welfare recipients to equal treatment under existing programs. See, for example, the "Spendthrift" guardianship laws which exist in almost one-fourth of the states, or *Wilkie v. O'Connor*, 261 App. Div. 373, 25 N.Y.S. 2d 617 (1941) which concluded that a welfare recipient had "no right to defy the standards and conventions of civilized society . . . at public expense."

Chapter 6

Treatment Alternatives: Goal and Reality

"... the only profession that labors incessantly to destroy the reason for its own existence."

As we examine the history of our social policy and the professions that have implemented that policy [Levine and Levine, 1970; Rothman, 1971], we discover an interesting pattern of change and adaptation. During periods when social institutions are responding to human needs and meeting national crises, such as the start of the Industrial Revolution or during the Second World War, problems of crime and mental illness are delegated to institutions de-

147

Treatment Alternatives: Goal and Reality

veloped specifically to meet those needs[1] During times of rapid social change when our social institutions have been less responsive to human need, such as the period of major immigration at the turn of the century or during the decades following World War II, the emphasis has been on the delegation of these responsibilities to the immediate community.

This pattern has an obvious logic to it, but it also has some unfortunate consequences. The United States has often been accused of a reluctance to experiment with promising alternative methods of meeting human and social needs. This is not supported by our social history. During the early nineteenth century, America provided full support to a movement designed to place the criminal and the mentally ill in the hands of professionals who were particularly qualified to provide the most progressive and humane treatment and rehabilitation. Society looked to the accomplishments of the Industrial Revolution, with its massive brick factories and productive specialization, and reasoned that this same professional specialization should be able to respond with equal success to human and social needs. This would take the mentally ill out of backrooms in communities that did not understand them and criminals out of local jails and place them in special environments where skilled professionals could prepare them to reenter the community as useful and productive citizens. The results included the progressive Ossining State Penitentiary, just up the Hudson from New York City, which has given us

148

the expression "up the river" and left us with "Sing Sing"; an institution that stands today.

America's nineteenth-century social institutions attracted international admiration. They provided sound treatment and individual attention and for close to two decades justified our recognition as an international leader in effective and humane rehabilitation policy. But times change. In our total commitment to programs, buildings, methods and personnel, we inadvertently plant the seeds of our own undoing. Gradually the institutions that served us well were asked to assume tasks for which they were not prepared and to respond to changes they could neither understand nor accept. When society is challenged by new and demanding social issues, it is often the commitment of its resources to outdated solutions that restricts its acceptance of new alternatives.

A commitment to community-oriented models does not of itself solve the dilemma. Virtually every "innovative," community-based program introduced during the past 20 years has its historical roots in eighteenth-century social policy or in programs introduced before the First World War. The colonial almshouse or Philadelphia's Walnut Street jail[2] would both be considered progressive community programs by today's standards and the modern multi-service center is indistinguishable in concept from the products of the settlement house movement. Rarely did any of these early predecessors survive for more than a generation or two.

149

Treatment Alternatives: Goal and Reality

The reason for the striking changes in the structure of our social institutions is in part because successful programs are built around people, not bricks and mortar. The imagination, skill, and dedication necessary to provide effective human services cannot be easily transferred. An equally important reason is that social needs change and with them our concept of the individual changes. When society sees its social institutions as adequately meeting human needs, it is inclined to view crime and mental illness as problems of the individual. When our institutions are not seen as meeting human needs, crime and mental illness are seen as products of society.

These distinct perspectives on the nature of human deviance have particular implication for the programs of correction and treatment which we prescribe. If we see crime or illness as an individual problem, then it becomes the responsibility of social institution to reshape the individual in order to prepare him to function in the larger society. If, on the other hand, we see deviate behavior as a response to social conditions, then we are inclined to protect the individual from society and develop alternative models for meeting his human needs.

The problem is that often in our eagerness to *do something*, we go entirely too far. This is complicated by the natural desire of members of the helping professions to do something *for* the people they serve and society's desire to maintain some measure of control *over* its social institutions and the particular public it serves. In the individual model of social deviance, the problem manifests itself in a ten-

150

dency to control or regiment the lives of those who come in contact with social institutions. In the Societal Model we tend to compensate the "victims" of social reality[3] and protect them from the problems of daily life. In both cases the burden of responsibility is shifted from the individual involved to the social institution. [Glazer, 1971].

Clearly there are times when it is necessary for a social institution to provide structure or support to the individuals who draw upon it. This, however, should be kept to a minimum; the inevitable consequence of prolonged structure is institutionalization, and the inevitable consequence of prolonged support is dependence. In both cases the outcome for the individual is determined by the institution. In this situation the individual can claim no responsibility for his success, and the institution must claim full responsibility for his failure. This is not a condition that is conducive to positive change. The most we could expect is that the individual would attempt to regain some measure of control over his own life. We have already examined some of the ways this can be done. We will examine others as we look at treatment alternatives.

Most of the current treatment modalities applied to the issue of drug abuse can be divided into two groups: medical maintenance models and self-help abstinence models [Brill and Lieberman, 1972]. In actuality the self-help models are group programs [Yablonsky, 1965] which have their origins in similar approaches which have been applied to alcoholism [Alcoholics Anonymous, 1955] and mental illness [Low, 1954]. These programs tend to be financially independent[4] and are operated by nonprofessional "ex-addicts." Members of these "therapeutic communities" function in a highly structured setting which emphasizes individual vulnerability to drugs and provides group settings in which common experiences are shared and abstinence is reinforced. The interpersonal dynamics are usually intense and often resemble a family composed entirely of children of different ages who are attempting to function effectively and responsibly in an adult world.

The medical maintenance approach is founded on a disease model and is typically operated by professionals. In most instances, maintenance programs are publically supported and in no case is a maintenance program controlled by "addicts." While some maintenance programs provide services other than drug support, which are geared to deal with other aspects of the "addict's" life, the basic assumption is that the individual suffers from a lifetime disease which has no cure and will require life-time "medication."

Both the abstinence model and the maintenance model are operated on the assumption that drugs are central to the life of the individual; the abstinence model assumes that the "addict" cannot return to the use of drugs without endangering his life, and the maintenance model assumes that he can never stop the use of drugs without the same consequence. Both assumptions are highly exaggerated.

Alcoholics Anonymous, for example, operates on the primary assumption that alcoholism is a disease and that even one drink will trigger the operation of that disease in a way that will make it impossible to resist the compulsive use of excessive amounts of alcohol. A research team at Johns Hopkins University School of Medicine [Bigelow, Cohen, Liebson, and Faillace, 1972] became interested in this "disease process" and tested the phenomenon in a group of chronic alcoholics. The subjects in their research were given access to substantial quantities of alcohol and told that they would be given an opportunity to participate in particular social and recreational activities if they drank in moderation:

> Traditional lore concerning alcoholism has suggested that alcoholics are unable to drink moderately—that once they start they are unable to stop. The present data specifically contradict this contention. . . . The fact that moderation is sustained in preference to abstinence suggests that moderation is the easier behavior to maintain. . . . [1972, p. 212]

On the other hand, the belief that narcotic withdrawal is a physical trauma on the order of denying insulin to a diabetic has no basis in medical fact. Even among chronic high-dose users, narcotic withdrawal is not as life-threatening as withdrawal from barbiturates[5] or even from alcohol. Major withdrawal symptoms generally last a few days, and noticeable recovery usually occurs within a week [GAP, 1971]. Complete recuperation may take up to six months, but it is not uncommon for workers to report the same symptoms for the same time period following a change to working a night shift.

Fortunately the problem is usually not even this severe.

Treatment Alternatives: Goal and Reality

Even during the period when high quality narcotics were more easily available, less than 20 percent of the users had habits severe enough to require detoxification [Kolb and Himmelsbach, 1938]. More recently, in Vietnam, almost every soldier had the opportunity to experiment with quality heroin and almost all personally knew other soldiers who used heroin with some regularity. This "natural experiment" provided the base for Lee Robins' extensive study of drug dependence among Vietnam veterans:

> Surprisingly, in the light of the common belief that dependence on narcotics is easily acquired and virtually impossible to rid oneself of, most of the men who used narcotics heavily and over a prolonged period in Vietnam stopped when they left Vietnam and had not begun again by the time of interview 8 to 12 months later. Perhaps even more surprising was the fact that of those who continued narcotic use after their return to the United States most reported that they had not become addicted or readdicted. Contrary to conventional belief, the occasional use of narcotics without becoming addicted appears to be possible even for men who have previously been dependent on narcotics. [Robins, 1973, p. 22]

Today, in the United States, the illegally available narcotic supply has become so thoroughly adulterated that it rarely contains enough active ingredients to produce physical dependence.[6] As Frederick Glaser has concluded:

> . . . the seriousness of the withdrawal symptoms, even for those few individuals actually dependent upon narcotics,

154

has been greatly exaggerated. An exhaustive search of the world literature revealed no instances of death due to uncomplicated withdrawal, and this was consonant with thirty years experience in withdrawal at Lexington. Clinical experience with users indicates that they exhibit severe withdrawal symptoms mainly when such an exhibition will lead to more medication, and that most are well aware of the essential mildness of the withdrawal syndrome. [1972, p. 21]

If the underlying assumptions of both major treatment modalities are clearly false, why are these particular modalities used most frequently and why do they seem to work when others fail? The answer to the first question is simple. Most of the people who now operate either abstinence or maintenance programs have tried other approaches and they have not worked. In fact, the major justification for the existence of maintenance programs is that although we can detoxify drug users with relatively little difficulty, people keep going back to drugs.

The answer to the second question is a bit more complicated and involves two separate considerations. First, it is clear that the treatment process itself is of some benefit to the individuals involved. Many people live with serious personal difficulties that they never fully understand nor are able to articulate. A person who can explain his fears and problems and deal with them on a verbal level can often benefit from other forms of psychotherapy. For a person who cannot, the global concept of "addiction" can serve as a focal point into which all other human problems can be directed. Again, in Epstein's words, "symptoms that substitute known for unknown fears." As long as this "diagnosis" can be confirmed and the condition "treated," the management of the underlying problems is less of an immediate concern.

William Schofield [1964] has characterized psychotherapy as the purchase of friendship. If this has any truth, it can certainly be applied to drug treatment programs as well. The self-help model is, in fact, an intense, structured social situation [Volkman and Cressey, 1963]. Unlike most forms of therapy, it is based on peer helping peer; each member of the community has an opportunity to give and receive help. While this model exacts a price in terms of an acceptance of both a high level of structure and an "addict" identity [Wechsler, 1960], many consider it a small price to pay for the benefits accrued.

The second part of the answer to why these modalities seem to work while others fail is, like the forest through the trees, sometimes difficult to recognize. The fact is that "addiction" is not really a disease as we know it; therefore it does not have to follow the rules of a disease. If a person is convinced he has a disease, it is not necessary for the disease to be "real" to effect a "cure." While the premise that an alcoholic cannot stop at one drink may be medically false, the corollary, "if I never take a drink I will not get drunk," can still be perfectly sound.

In the last analysis the use of drugs is like any intense human or physical experience; it leaves a mark, good or bad; whatever else you may do, it will never be forgotten.

Treatment Alternatives: Goal and Reality

People live with the important experiences of their past in one of two ways—they continue the experience or they do not. All of the lengthy literature on the treatment of addiction ultimately comes down to the same thing: maintenance or abstinence. The concept of "cure" is a myth. The question for the individual and for society is whether the life each person builds out of his or her experience is constructive or destructive.

During the past decade we have witnessed an increasing recognition of the need for new social institutions to respond to the needs of our criminal justice system. Our current penal system is the remnant of a structure designed to meet the needs of a different era and a different concept of human existence. The alternatives we seek today stem from the realization that the primary responsibility of society is to assure every citizen the opportunity to develop his or her maximum potential.

One alternative that has grown from this realization is the concept of pretrial diversion.[7] Pre-trial diversion provides an alternative to incarceration for eligible offenders who decide to accept that opportunity. As the justice administration system became increasingly involved with drug-related cases, it has looked to pre-trial diversion as an alternative that could serve the best interests of both the individual drug user and the larger society. The results have been less than completely successful [Robertson, 1972].

Alternative models of justice administration offer an obvious appeal and a genuine potential in responding to

157

criminal justice aspects of the drug issue. It is critical, however, that the formulation of an alternative model include a careful evaluation of the special issues surrounding "addiction" and a recognition of the historical relationship between the medical and legal professions. Offenders come to pre-trial diversion with sophisticated rationalizations for their criminal behavior. Dealing with these rationalizations is the first responsibility of the program, and ultimately most offenders learn to accept the responsibility for their actions. Those who do not return to court to face their charges.

The drug-related offender is often a very different story. The deviance of crime and the deviance of illicit drug use both stem from and support a separation from the mainstream of social values. The systems of rationalizations seen among drug users are typically complex and firmly entrenched. Usually arrest itself is seen as a verification of these rationalizations, and the alternatives offered to the drug user are often seen as one more opportunity for manipulation. Complicating all of these factors is a physiological or psychogenic dependence on a drug which in itself is a significant barrier to communication.

Society has taught the illicit drug user that he is a victim of a disease and that disease is seen as a proof of still other inequities. The fact that society seeks additionally to hold the user of illicit drugs responsible for his criminal actions provides the final nail in an often impenetrable wall.

Our legal and social institutions have contributed to the dilemma. We have sought to enforce control in the name of treatment and to shield men from their responsibilities in the name of rehabilitation. Both approaches violate the letter and spirit of professional ethics and national policy. In our eagerness to find *some* solution to a social problem, we have failed to consider what other professions also had to learn through hard experience. The physical-health professions lived through a period when they too sought to protect the handicapped from the realities of their physical limitations and in so doing condemned a significant portion of our population to dependence and isolation. Urban policy analysts are only now recognizing that the realities we once considered liabilities can actually form the basis for a new and strong direction in public policy [Thompson, 1965; Turner and Fichter, 1972].

Only rarely have we seen instances in which justice administration and social service programs have combined their talents in a coordinated effort based on the assumption that adults can and must accept their social responsibilities. These instances have, however, demonstrated the potential of this approach [Glasser, 1965; Vaillant, 1966; Brill and Lieberman, 1969; Edwards, Calhoun, Mello, and Coakley, 1972]. During the Second World War military psychiatry adopted a policy of removing troops from the front lines if they displayed symptoms of psychiatric disturbance. One theory was that these disturbances were the result of physical trauma, or "shell shock," caused by exploding munitions, and the soldiers were considered victims of a physical injury. Out of kindness, we returned them to veterans' hospitals for proper treatment, where many of them are today. The First Army in Europe lost 10 percent of its troops to psychiatric casualties during the height of World War II. By the time of Vietnam, we recognized that "shell shock" was a myth. Through effective training, preventive psychiatry, and a policy of treating psychiatric problems in the field, the psychiatric casualty rate was reduced to 1 percent [Allerton, 1969].

If we are to respond effectively to the drug issue, we must first deal with the basis for rationalizations which make confrontation of the problem so very difficult. Treatment programs cannot serve as an instrument of social control. The justice administration system is justified in intervening in the life of an offender only on the basis of established violation of a duly enacted and constitutionally valid law. If the community, through its judicial representatives, considers that a case involves sufficient extenuating circumstances to warrant acquittal, then it must make that decision within the bounds of law. In no instance can that decision be legitimately determined on the basis of the defendant's status as an "addict." If the court determines that it has no grounds for criminal action, the defendant's status as an "addict" should not form the basis of an alternative disposition, and no responsible service program should accept a judicial referral made under those conditions.

If, on the other hand, the court determines that it is justified in taking criminal action, then the status of "addiction" should not influence the court's disposition. It is clear, however, that both the individual offender and society at large would benefit from the availability of a dispositional alternative which would satisfy the community's sense of justice and also provide the highest possible level of service to the offender.[8] If we operate within this framework, the creation of that alternative becomes a realistic possibility.

The justice administration system has not begun to exhaust its possible effective and innovative alternatives. The concept of restitution offers great promise of properly applied, but experimentation with the concept is only in its infancy [Fogel, Galaway, and Hudson, 1972]. Community-based corrections offer genuine promise if they remain responsive to their commitment and adapt to social change. Both pre-trial and post-trial diversion can be operated in residential and nonresidential settings.

The success of each of these alternatives rests, however, on the condition that every party involved clearly understand the responsibilities and limitations of their respective roles [Thomas, 1963]. Human service programs are subject to a wide array of internal and external pressures, and program failure can usually be attributed to an inability to respond appropriately to these subtle forces [Polsky, Claster, and Goldberg, 1970]. But most important is the constant recognition that the human services cannot use their professional position to circumvent the prevailing legal and moral climate of the community. Human service professionals, no less than any other member of the community, have a right and a responsibility to apply their beliefs and experience to the shaping of social policy. Human service professionals also have an obligation, no less than that of other professions, to recognize and support the foundations of our judicial system.[9] Inevitably in a democratic society, it is the community and constitutional interpretation that defines prevailing justice.

Notes

1. Examination of the history of addiction will also demonstrate that addiction and other forms of deviance also spontaneously decline during these periods.

2. See Rothman [1971, p. 54].

3. You may recall the now-famous line from *West Side Story:* "I'm depraved 'cause I was deprived."

4. This is particularly true of Alcoholics Anonymous and Recovery, Inc., which, as the names imply, are private organizations which neither seek publicity (other than to recruit membership) or want outside financial or professional control. *Synanons* began under similar guidelines but now accept referrals and public financial support while retaining private control.

5. Contrary to popular belief, the most difficult withdrawal picture is presented by the combined barbiturate-amphetamine dependence.

6. One virtue of the present drug laws is that they have kept the active ingredient content of street drugs at a much lower level than is commonly available through maintenance programs. The disadvantage, of course, is that the level of impurities is correspondingly higher in street drugs.

7. See, for example, the *Boston Court Resource Project.* Bedford, Mass: Technical Development Corporation, 1973.

8. Not surprisingly, drug use is found to decline after users experience positive change in other areas of their lives.

9. This concept is incorporated into the position reports of most professional human service organizations. See, for example, Horman and Fox [1970].

Chapter 7 Responding to the Challenge: A Look to the Future

"Most of the change we think we see in life Is due to truth's being in and out of favor."[1]

—*Robert Frost*

In their attempt to know and understand the experiences that shape and challenge them, men often elect a course of action which affects the perception and consequences of experiences in a way nature never intended and fact cannot support. In our attempt to know and understand the drug phenomenon, we have taken such a course. Drug use is a difficult experience to understand. In our efforts to control drug use and treat the drug user, we have

165

looked on drug use as both a crime and a disease. The available medical evidence and the best legal interpretation support neither viewpoint.

In the hope of dealing with the drug issue we have tried to turn the medical profession into judicial arbitrators and the courts into psychiatrists. Drug abuse has become a topic of political and policy debate and has challenged the foundations of every major social institution. We have told the drug user he is both villain and a victim. We offer him help at the expense of dependence and provide control which perpetuates contempt. In an effort to draw the drug user back into the community, we have isolated him from society and perpetuated his irresponsibility.

In the attempt to shape our social institutions to a new and difficult challenge, it is easy to forget their original intent and to erode the human and structural elements which give each institution its own particular strength and purpose. Many of our fears about drug abuse and our concerns about social institutions have become self-fulfilling prophecies. The challenge we now face demands the revitalization of each of our social institutions and a renewed dedication to their respective duties and responsibilities.

Few of the stereotypes and generalizations about drug abuse can be supported in fact. All of the labels we have applied to drug use undoubtedly apply to some drug users. Some drug users are clearly criminals, but crime cannot be realistically interpreted as either the cause or the consequence of drug abuse. Some users are mentally ill, others both medically and legally insane. But there is no basis for assuming that drug use is either a cause or a verification of mental illness. The only valid generalization is that drug use is a behavior and that drug "addiction" is a status.

Our society has evolved a system of human and medical care and a system of justice administration. Both systems are overworked and understaffed. Both must be improved if they are to meet the contemporary needs of the communities they serve. At the same time, we must not forget that each system has a unique responsibility and is built on a foundation which is designed to serve that responsibility. These systems provide us with three legitimate and constitutionally valid points of individual intervention in our response to the social issue of drug abuse:

1. If the individual is a minor or otherwise subject to legal guardianship, then the right and responsibility for intervention is delegated by law to the parent or legal guardian. The alternative courses of action and avenues of legal recourse open to the parent or guardian are identical to those relating to other areas of conduct.

2. If the individual is unable to accurately evaluate the existence and consequences of relevant alternatives, the state may initiate civil commitment procedures. However, under no circumstances can the status of addiction or disagreement with the suggested course of treatment constitute in and of themselves grounds for concluding that the individual comes under the legal jurisdiction of civil commitment. In every case, the state or other initiating party must recognize that their actions will be subject to constitutional interpretation. The use of involuntary civil commit-

ment as a method of social regulation violates the spirit of our national heritage *and* our constitutional tradition. The probability that civil commitment will endure the letter of the law is slight.

3. If an individual has violated a duly enacted and constitutionally valid law, the community, through its judicial representatives, has the right and responsibility to take whatever action it deems appropriate in light of its prevailing judgment and beliefs. In no instance, however, can the status of "addiction" be assumed to constitute grounds for mitigation or grounds for the imposition of special sanctions.

Our justice administration system is experiencing a period of growth and change. During this period it will and must develop alternative models for providing the convicted offender with both an opportunity to pay his debt to society and to develop his own human potential. These alternatives, however, cannot be allowed to evolve into a method of circumventing the prevailing judgment of the community or providing a means of social regulation in the name of involuntary therapeutic treatment. The drug-dependent offender, as surely as all other offenders, must be given a meaningful opportunity to make decisions which govern his own life and must be held responsible for the consequences of those decisions.

Notes

1. From "The Black Cottage," from *The Poetry of Robert Frost* edited by Edward Connery Lathem. Copyright 1930, 1939, © 1969 by Holt, Rinehart and Winston, Inc. Copyright © 1958 by Robert Frost. Copyright © 1967 by Lesley Frost Ballantine. Reprinted by permission of Holt, Rinehart and Winston, Inc.

References

Abood, L. G. The biochemistry of psychoactive drugs. In R. E. Horman and A. M. Fox (Eds.) *Drug awareness*. New York: Avon Books, 1970. Pp. 56–66.

Ackerman, N. W. Prejudicial scapegoating and neutralizing forces in the family group, with special reference to the role of "family healer." In J. G. Howells (Ed.) *Theory and practice of family psychiatry*. New York: Brunner/Mazel, 1971. Pp. 626–634.

Adams, J. S. Inequity in social exchange. In L. Berkowitz (Ed.) *Advances in experimental social psychology*. New York: Academic Press, 1965.

Alcoholics Anonymous. *Alcoholics anonymous*. New York: Alcoholics Anonymous Publishing, 1955.

Alexander, F. and Staub, H. *The criminal, the judge, and the public*. (Rev. ed.) Glencoe, Ill.: The Free Press, 1956.

Alinsky, S. D. *Rules for radicals*. New York: Random House, 1971.

Allerton, W. S. Army psychiatry in Viet Nam. In P. G. Bourne (Ed.) *The psychology and physiology of stress*. New York: Academic Press, 1969.

Allport, G. W. *Pattern and growth in personality*. New York: Holt, Rinehart and Winston, 1937.

171

References

AMA Committee on Alcoholism and Drug Dependence. *Drug Dependence: A Guide for Physicians.* Chicago: American Medical Association, 1970.

AMA Council on Mental Health. Review of the operation of narcotic "clinics" between 1919 and 1923. In J. A. O'Donnell and J. C. Ball (Eds.) *Narcotic addiction.* New York: Harper and Row, 1966. Pp. 180–187.

American Friends Service Committee. *Struggle for justice.* New York: Hill and Wang, 1971.

Aronowitz, D. Civil commitment of narcotic addicts. *Columbia Law Review,* 1967, *67* (3), 405–429.

Ash, P. The reliability of psychiatric diagnoses. *Journal of Abnormal Social Psychology,* 1949, *44,* 272–277.

Ausubel, D. P. Controversial issues in the management of drug addiction: Legalization, ambulatory treatment, and the British System. In J. A. O'Donnell and J. C. Ball (Eds.) *Narcotic addiction.* New York: Harper and Row, 1966, Pp. 195–209.

Bach, R. *Stranger to the ground.* New York: Harper and Row, 1963.

Balter, M. B. and Levine, J. The nature and extent of psychotropic drug use in the United States. *Psychopharmacology Bulletin,* 1969, *5*(4), 1–13.

Bakewell, W. E. and Wikler, A. Nonnarcotic addiction: incidence in a university hospital psychiatric ward. *Journal American Medical Association,* 1966, *196,* 122–125.

Barber, T. X. *LSD, marijuana, yoga and hypnosis.* Chicago: Aldine, 1970.

References

Becker, H. S. Becoming a marihuana user. *American Journal of Sociology*, 1953, *59*, 235–242.

Beecher, H. K. Nonspecific forces surrounding disease and the treatment of disease. *Journal American Medical Association*, 1962, *179*, 137–140.

Beecher, H. K. Placebo effects of situations, attitudes, and drugs: a quantitative study of suggestibility. In K. Rickels (Ed.) *Nonspecific factors in drug therapy*. Springfield, Ill: C. C. Thomas, 1968.

Bejerot, N. An epidemic of phenmetrazine dependence—epidemiological and clinical aspects. In C. W. M. Wilson (Ed.) *Pharmacological and epidemiological aspects of adolescent drug dependence*. Oxford: Pergamon Press, 1968. Pp. 55–66.

Bejerot, N. *Addiction: An artificially induced drive*. Springfield, Ill: C. C. Thomas, 1972.

Bennett, D. E. Marihuana use among college students and street people. Harvard University: Unpublished senior honors thesis, 1971.

Berscheid, E. and Walster, E. When does a harm-doer compensate a victim? *Journal of Personality and Social Psychology*, 1967, *6*(4), 435–441.

Bigelow, G., Cohen, M., Liebson, I., and Faillace, L. A. Abstinence or moderation? choice by alcoholics. *Behavior Research and Therapy*, 1972, *10*, 209–214.

Biggs, J., Jr. *The guilty mind: psychiatry and the law of homicide*. New York: Harcourt, Brace and Co., 1955.

Blau, P. M. *Exchange and power in social life*. New York: Wiley, 1967.

References

Blum, R. H. and Associates. *Society and drugs*. San Francisco: Jossey-Bass, 1970(a).

Blum, R. H. and Associates. *Students and drugs*. San Francisco: Jossey-Bass, 1970(b).

Blum, R. H. and Associates. *The dream sellers*. San Francisco: Jossey-Bass, 1972(a).

Blum, R. H. and Associates. *Horatio Alger's children*. San Francisco: Jossey-Bass, 1972(b).

Bond, D. D. *The love and fear of flying*. New York: International Universities Press, 1952.

Bourne, P. G. *Men, stress, and Vietnam*. Boston: Little, Brown, 1970.

Brecher, E. M. *Licit and illicit drugs*. Boston: Little, Brown, 1972.

Brill, H. and Larimore, G. W. *Second on-site study of the British narcotic system*. Albany, N. Y.: New York State Narcotic Control Commission, 1968.

Brill, L. and Lieberman, L. *Authority and addiction*. Boston: Little Brown, 1969.

Brill, L. and Lieberman, L. (Eds.) *Major modalities in the treatment of drug abuse*. New York: Behavioral Publications, 1972.

Brownfield, C. A. *Isolation: Clinical and experimental approaches*. New York: Random House, 1965.

Butler, J. R. Illness and the sick role: An evaluation in three communities. *British Journal of Sociology*, 1970, *21* (3), 241–261.

Cannon, W. B. Voodoo death. *American Anthropology*, 1942, *44*, 2.

References

Cannon, W. B. *Bodily changes in pain, hunger, fear, and rage*. New York: Harper and Row, 1963.

Casper, E. W. Jurors review mental illness: A review of the literature. *Pennsylvania Psychiatric Quarterly*, 1964, 4(2), 63–67.

Chayet, N. L. *Legal implications of emergency care*. New York: Appleton-Century-Crofts, 1969.

Chein, I., Gerard, D. L., Lee, R. S., and Rosenfeld, E. *The road to H: Narcotics, delinquency and social policy*. New York: Basic Books, 1964.

Christopher, M. *ESP, seers and psychics*. New York: Crowell, 1970.

Civil commitment of narcotics addicts. *Yale Law Journal*, 1967, 76(6), 1160–1189.

Committee on Nomenclature and Statistics of the American Psychiatric Association. *Diagnostic and statistical manual of mental disorders (DSM-II)*. Washington: American Psychiatric Association, 1968.

Cowan, R. C. American conservatives should revise their position on marijuana. *National Review*, December 8, 1972, 1344–1346.

Cressey, D. R. Role theory, differential association, and compulsive crimes. In D. R. Cressey and D. A. Ward (Eds.) *Delinquency, crime, and social process*. New York: Harper and Row, 1969. Pp. 1114–1128.

Curran, W. J. Tort liability of the mentally ill and mentally deficient. *Ohio State Law Journal*, 1960, 21(1), 52–74.

Cutting, W. C. *Drug hazards in aviation medicine*. Washington: Federal Aviation Administration, 1962.

References

Darling, R. C. High altitude sickness. In Beeson, P. B. and McDermott, W. (Eds.) *Medicine*. Philadelphia: Saunders, 1963. Pp. 1813–1815.

Davidson, C. and Silverstone, T. Diuretic dependence. *British Medical Journal*, 1972, *1*, 505.

Davidson, H. A. Criminal responsibility: the quest for a formula. In P. H. Hoch & J. Zabin (Eds.) *Psychiatry and the law*. New York: Grune & Stratton, 1955. Pp. 61–70.

Davison, G. C. and Valins, S. Maintenance of self-attributed and drug-attributed behavior change. *Journal of Personality and Social Psychology* 1969, *11*(1), 25–33.

Defleur, L. and Garrett, G. Dimensions of marihuana usage in land-grant universities. *Journal of Counseling Psychology*, 1970, *17*, 468–476.

Dole, V. Biochemistry of addiction. *Annual Review of Biochemistry*, 1970, *39*, 821–840.

Dole, V. P. and Nyswander, M. E. A medical treatment for diacetyl-morphine (heroin) addiction. *Journal of the American Medical Association*, 1965, *193*(8), 646–650.

Dole, V. P. and Nyswander, M. E. Heroin addiction—a metabolic disease. *Archives of Internal Medicine*, 1967, *120*, 19–24.

Dumont, M. P. Drug problems and their treatment: Organization of programs at the state and local level. In G. Caplan (Ed.) *The American handbook of psychiatry*, Vol. III. (Rev. ed.) New York: Basic Books, 1972.

Dunbar, F. *Emotions and bodily changes*. New York: Columbia University Press, 1954.

References

Dunbar, F. *Psychiatry in the medical specialties*. New York: McGraw-Hill, 1959.

Edwards, C. N. Drugs and youth, *Harvard Educational Review*, 1972, *42* (4), 572–578.

Edwards, C. N., Calhoun, J., Mello, E., and Coakley, R. *The selection and training of advocates and screeners for a pre-trial diversion program*. Boston: Boston Court Resource Project, 1972.

Edwards, C. N. Interactive styles and social adaptation. *Genetic Psychology Monographs*, 1973, *87*, 123–174.

Eldridge, W. B. *Narcotics and the law: A critique of the American experiment in narcotic drug control*. New York: American Bar Foundation, 1962.

Elkin, F. Specialists interpret the case of Harry Holzer. *Journal of Abnormal Social Psychology*, 1947, *42*, 99–111.

Ennis, B. J. The rights of mental patients. In N. Dorsen (Ed.) *The rights of Americans*. New York: Pantheon Books, 1971. Pp. 484–498.

Epstein, S. Toward a unified theory of anxiety. In B. A. Maher (Ed.) *Progress in experimental personality research*, Vol. 4, V. New York: Academic Press, 1967.

Erikson, K. T. Patient role and social uncertainty—a dilemma of the mentally ill. *Psychiatry*, 1957, *20*, 263–274.

Essig, C. F. Addiction to nonbarbiturate sedative and tranquilizing drugs. *Clinical and Pharmacological Therapeutics*, 1964, *5*, 334–343.

Ewing, J. A. and Bakewell, W. E. Diagnosis and management of depressant drug dependence. *American Journal of Psychiatry*, 1967, *123*, 909–917.

References

Feuer, L. S. *The conflict of generations*. New York: Basic Books, 1969.

Fishbein, M. The relationships between beliefs, attitudes, and behavior. In Shel Feldman (Ed.) *Cognitive Consistency*. New York: Academic Press, 1966. Pp. 199–223.

Fogel, D., Galaway, B., and Hudson, J. Restitution in criminal justice: a Minnesota experiment. *Criminal Law Bulletin*, 1972, *8*(8), 681–691.

Fort, J. *The pleasure seekers: the drug crisis, youth and society*. New York: Grove Press, 1969.

GAP Committee on Mental Health Services. *Drug misuse: A psychiatrict view of a modern dilemma*. New York: Charles Scribner's Sons, 1971.

Garrison, P. Why we fly. *Flying*, 1972, *90*, 38–39.

Gibbons, D. C. Crime and punishment: A study in social attitudes. *Social Forces*, 1969, *47*(4), 391–397.

Glaser, F. B. Is methadone maintenance preferable to withdrawal? *International Journal of Offender Therapy and Comparative Criminology*, 1972, *16*(1), 18–24.

Glasser, W. *Reality Therapy*. New York: Harper and Row, 1965.

Glazer, N. The limits of social policy. *Commentary*, 1971, *52*(3), 51–58.

Glueck, S. *Mental disorder and the criminal law*. Boston: Little, Brown, 1925.

Glueck, S. *Law and psychiatry*. Baltimore: John Hopkins Press, 1962.

Goffman, E. *Stigma*. Englewood Cliffs, N.J.: Prentice-Hall, 1963.

References

Goffman, E. Where the action is. In E. Goffman. *Interaction ritual.* New York: Doubleday, 1967.

Goldstein, A. The pharmacologic basis of methadone treatment. Paper presented at the Fourth National Conference on Methadone Treatment, San Francisco, January 8–10, 1972.

Goldstein, J., and Katz, J. Abolish the "insanity defense"—why not? *Yale Law Journal*, 1963, 72(5), 853–876.

Goodman, L. and Gilman, A. *The pharmacological basis of therapeutics.* New York: Macmillan, 1955.

Graubard, M. The Frankenstein syndrome: Man's ambivalent attitude to knowledge and power. *Perspectives in Biology and Medicine*, 1967, 10(3), 419–443.

Great Britain, Scottish Home and Health Department. *Drug addiction: The second report of the interdepartmental committee.* London: Her Majesty's Stationery Office, 1967. (Second Brain Report)

Greenblatt, D. J. and Shader, R. I. Meprobamate: A study of irrational drug use. *American Journal of Psychiatry*, 1971, 127(10), 1297–1303.

Greenblott, B. M. Mental disorder and the criminal law. Harvard University: Unpublished senior honors thesis, 1967.

Grinspoon, L. *Marijuana reconsidered*, Cambridge: Harvard University Press, 1971.

Guttmacher, M. S. Criminal responsibility in certain homicide cases involving family members. In P. H. Hoch and J. Zubin (Eds.) *Psychiatry and the law*. New York: Grune and Stratton, 1955, p. 73–96.

179

References

Guttmacher, M. S. The psychiatrist as an expert witness. *University of Chicago Law Review*, 1955, *22*, 325–330.

Hager, D. L., Vener, A. M., and Stewart, C. S. Patterns of adolescent drug use in Middle America. *Journal of Counseling Psychology*, 1971, *18*(4), 292–297.

Hart, H. L. A. and Honore, A. M. Causation in the law. *Law Quarterly Review*, 1956, 72(1), 58–90.

Hartung, F. E. A vocabulary of motives for law violations. In D. R. Cressey and D. A. Ward (Eds.) *Delinquency, crime and social process*. New York: Harper and Row, 1969, Pp. 454–473.

Heath, R. G. Electrical self-stimulation of the brain in man. *American Journal of Psychiatry*, 1963, *120*, 571–577.

Heyman, F. Methadone maintenance as law and order. *Society*, 1972, *9*,(8), 15–25.

Hirst, D. V. Contraceptive tablets and emotional states. *Obstetrics and gynecology*, 1971, *38*(1), 147–151.

Hollister, L. E., Motzenbecker, F. P., and Degan, R. O. Withdrawal reactions from Chlordiazepoxide ("Librium"). *Psychopharmacologia*, 1961, *2*, 63–68.

Homans, G. C. *The human group*. New York: Harcourt, Brace & World, 1950.

Honigfeld, G. Nonspecific factors in treatment. *Diseases Nervous System*, 1964, *25*, 145–156.

Horman, R. and Fox. A. (Eds.) *Drug awareness*. New York: Avon Books, 1970.

References

Houts, M. *They asked for death*. New York: Cowles Book Co., 1970.

Hovland, C. I., Janis, I. L., and Kelley, H. H. *Communication and persuasion: Psychological studies of opinion change*. New Haven and London: Yale University Press, 1953.

Hughes, G. Omissions and *mens reas*. In H. Morris (Ed.) *Freedom and responsibility*. Stanford: Stanford University Press, 1961. Pp. 226–230.

Isbell, H. Opium poisoning. In P. B. Beeson and W. McDermott (Eds.) *Medicine*. Philadelphia: Saunders, 1963. Pp. 1744–1749.

Isbell, H. and Chrusciel, T. L. Dependence liability of "non-narcotic" drugs. *Bulletin of the World Health Organization (Supplement)*, 1970.

Joint Committee of the American Bar Association and the American Medical Association on Narcotic Drugs. *Drug addiction: Crime or disease?* Bloomington, Ind.: Indiana University Press, 1961.

Jokl, E. and McClellan, J. T. Sudden cardiac death of pilots in flight. *Medicine and Sport*, 1971, *5*, 25–63.

Kalven, H., Jr., The jury, the law and the personal injury damage award. *Ohio State Law Journal*, 1958, *19*, 158–178.

Kaplan, J. *Marijuana: The new prohibition*. New York: World Publishing, 1970.

Katz, M. M. What this country needs is a safe five-cent intoxicant. *Psychology Today*, 1971, *4*(9), 28–94.

Kelley, H. H. Attribution theory in social psychology. In D. Levine (Ed.) 1967 *Nebraska Symposium on Motivation*. Lincoln: University of Nebraska Press, 1967.

References

Kelley, H. H. Interpersonal accomodation. *American Psychologist*, 1968, *23*(6), 339–410.

Kerckhoff, A. C. and Back, K. W. *The june bug: A study in hysterical contagion*. New York: Appleton-Century-Crofts, 1968.

Kety, S. S. Neurochemical aspects of emotional behavior. In P. Black (Ed.) *Physiological correlates of emotion*. New York: Academic Press, 1970., Pp. 61–71.

King, F. W. Marijuana and LSD usage among male college students: Prevalence rate, frequency, and self-estimates of future use. *Psychiatry*, 1969, *32*, 265–276.

Kolb, L. Drug addiction in its relation to crime. *Mental Hygiene*, 1925(a), *9*, 74–89.

Kolb, L. Pleasure and deterioration from narcotic addiction. *Mental Hygiene*, 1925(b), *9*, 699–724.

Kolb, L. and Himmelsbach, C. K. Clinical studies of drug addiction: A critical review of the withdrawal treatments with method of evaluating abstinence syndromes. *Public Health Report Supplement No. 128*. Washington: U.S. Government Printing Office, 1938.

Kramer, J. The state versus the addict: Uncivil commitment. *Boston University Law Review*, 1970, *50*(1), 1–22.

Kuh, R. H. A prosecutor considers the model penal code. *Columbia Law Review*, 1963, *63*(4), 608–631.

LaBarre, W. The narcotic complex of the New World. *Diogenes*, 1964, *48*, 125–138.

Laing, R. D. *The politics of experience*. New York: Ballantine, 1968.

References

Lasagna, L., von Felsinger, J. M., and Beecher, H. K. Drug-induced mood changes in man. *Journal American Medical Association*, 1955, *157*, 1006–1113.

Lauria, D. B. *The drug scene*. New York: McGraw-Hill, 1968.

Leblanc, J. Adaptive mechanisms in humans. *Annals of the New York Academy of Sciences*, 1966, *134*(2), 721–732.

Leifer, R. The competence of the psychiatrist to assist in the determination of incompetency. *Syracuse Law Review*, 1963, *14*(4), 564–575.

Lemere, F. Habit-forming properties of Meprobamate. *Archives of Neurology and Psychiatry*, 1956, *76*, 205–206.

Lennard, H. L., Epstein, L. J., and Rosenthal, M. S. The methadone illusion. *Science*, 1972, *176*, 881–884.

Levine, M. and Levine, A. *A social history of the helping services: Clinic, court, school and community*. New York: Appleton-Century-Crofts, 1970.

Levitt, A. Extent and function of the doctrine of *mens rea*. *Illinois Law Review*, 1928, *17*(8), 578–595.

Lindesmith, A. R. *The addict and the law*. Bloomington, Ind.: Indiana University Press, 1965.

Lindesmith, A. R. Basic problems in the social psychology of addiction and a theory. In J. A. O'Donnell and J. C. Ball (Eds.) *Narcotic addiction*. New York: Harper and Row, 1966.

Linsky, A. S. Theories of behavior and the image of the alcoholic in popular magazines, 1960–1966. *Public Opinion Quarterly*, 1970–1971 (Win.), *34*(4), 573–591.

References

Lipset, S. M. American student activism in comparative perspective. *American Psychologist*, 1970, *25*(8), 675–693.

Love, D. R., Brown, J. J., Fraser R., Lever, A. F., Robertson, J. I. S., Timbury, G. C., Thomson, S., and Tree, M. An unusual case of self-induced electrolyte depletion. *Gut*, 1971, *12*, 284–290.

Low, A. A. *Mental health through will training.* Boston: Christopher Publishing House, 1954.

Macniven, A. Psychoses and criminal responsibility. In H. Morris (Ed.) *Freedom and responsibility.* Stanford: Stanford University Press, 1961, Pp. 396–410.

Mahon, T. A. The British system, past and present. *International Journal of the Addictions*, 1971, *6*(4), 627–634.

Mandell, A. J. Neurochemical aspects of narcotic addiction. Paper presented at the Fourth National Conference on Methadone Treatment, San Francisco, January 8–10, 1972.

Marchbanks, V. H. Effects of flying stress on urinary 17-hydroxycorticosteroid levels. *Journal of Aviation Medicine*, 1958, *29*, 676–682.

Masserman, J. H. *The practice of dynamic psychiatry.* Philadelphia: W. B. Saunders, 1955.

Mauss, A. L. Anticipatory socialization toward college as a factor in adolescent marijuana use. *Social Problems*, 1969, *16*(3), 357–364.

Mauss, M. *The gift: Forms and functions of exchange in archaic societies.* Glencoe, Ill.: Free Press, 1954.

McGlothlin, W. H., Arnold, D. O., and Rowan, P. K. Marijuana use among adults. *Psychiatry*, 1970, *33*(4), 433–443.

References

McMorris, S. C. Can we punish for the acts of addiction? *Bulletin on Narcotics*, 1970, 22(3), 43–48.

Mehlman, B. The reliability of psychiatric diagnoses. *Journal of Abnormal Social Psychology*, 1952, 47, 577–578.

Mizner, G. L., Barter, J. T., and Werme, P. H. Patterns of drug use among college students: A preliminary report. *American Journal of Psychiatry*, 1970. 127(1), 15–24.

Mott, P. E., Mann, F. C., McLoughlin, Q., and Warick, D. P. *Shift work*. Ann Arbor: University of Michigan Press, 1965.

Moynihan, D. P. *Maximum feasible misunderstanding*. New York: Free Press, 1969.

Nutrition Committee, Canadian Pediatric Society. The use and abuse of vitamin A. *Canadian Medical Association Journal*, 1971, 104, 521–522.

Nyswander, M. Drug addictions. In S. Arieti (Ed.) *American handbook of psychiatry*. New York: Basic Books, 1959. Pp. 614–622.

O'Donnell, J. A. *Narcotics addicts in Kentucky*. U.S. Public Health Service Publication No. 1881. Chevy Chase, Md.: National Institute of Mental Health, 1969.

Olds, J. Self-stimulation of the brain. *Science*, 1958, 127, 315–324.

Overholser, W. *The psychiatrist and the law*. New York: Harcourt, Brace, & World, 1953.

Owen, D. E. *British opium policy in China and India*. New Haven: Yale University Press, 1968.

185

References

Patch, V. D. Methadone maintenance and crime reduction in Boston. Paper presented at the International Congress on Alcoholism and Addiction, Amsterdam, The Netherlands, September 7, 1972.

Perkins, R. M. *Cases and materials in criminal law and procedure*. (4th ed.) Mineola, N.Y.: Foundation Press, 1972.

Polenz, M. J. and Feder, S. L. Psychotherapeutic drugs-patterns of use. *Journal of the Mount Sinai Hospital, New York*, 1968, *35*, 246–257.

Polsky, S. Applications and limits of diminished responsibility as a legal and medical concept. In P. H. Hoch and J. Zubin (Eds.) *Psychiatry and the law*. New York: Grune and Stratton, 1955. Pp. 196–212.

Polsky, H. W., Claster, D. S., and Goldberg, C. (Eds.) *Social system perspectives in residential institutions*. East Lansing, Mich.: Michigan State University Press, 1970.

President's Commission on Law Enforcement and Administration of Justice. *The challenge of crime in a free society: A report by the president's commission on law enforcement and administration of justice*. Washington, D.C.: U.S. Government Printing Office, 1967.

Purgatives. *British Medical Journal*, 1969, *4*, 543–544.

Rector, M. G. Heroin maintenance: A rational approach. *Crime and Delinquency*, 1972, *18*(3), 241–242.

Robertson, J. A. Pre-trial diversion of drug offenders: A statutory approach. *Boston University Law Review*, 1972, *52*(2), 335–371.

Robins, L. N. An actuarial evaluation of the causes and consequences of deviant behavior in young black men. In R. Merrill, L. N. Robins and M. Pollack (Eds.) *Life history research in psychopathology*, Vol. II Minneapolis: University of Minnesota Press, 1972.

Robins, L. N. A follow-up of Vietnam drug users. Interim Final Report, 1973, Washington University, Contract No. HSM-42-72-75, Special Action Office for Drug Abuse Prevention.

Robins, L. N. and Murphy, G. E. Drug use in a normal population of young negro men. *American Journal of Public Health*, 1967, *57*, 1580–1596.

Roche, P. Q. *The criminal mind: A study of communication between the criminal law and psychiatry*. New York: Farrar, Straus and Cudahy, 1958.

Rock, P. E. Observations on debt collection. *British Journal of Sociology*, 1968, *19*(2), 176–190.

Rosen, P. L. *The supreme court and social science*. Urbana: University of Illinois Press, 1972.

Rosenzweig, N., Vandenberg, S. G., Moore, K., and Dukay, A. A study of the reliability of the mental status examination. *American Journal of Psychiatry*, 1961, *117*, 1102–1108.

Rothman, D. J. *The discovery of the asylum*. Boston: Little, Brown, 1971.

Rousell, C. H. and Edwards, C. N. Some developmental antecedents of psychopathology, *Journal of Personality*, 1971, *39*(3), 362–377.

Sayre, F. B. *Mens Rea. Harvard Law Review*, 1932, *45*(6), 974–1026.

Schachter, S. and Singer, J. E. Cognitive, social and psychological determinants of emotional state. *Psychological Review*, 1962, *69*, 379–399.

References

Schanberg, S. M., Schildkraut, J. J., and Kopin, I. J. The effects of psychoactive drugs on norepinephrine H3 metabolism in brain. *Biochemical Pharmacology*, 1967, *16*, 393–400.

Scheff, T. J. Negotiating reality: Notes on power in the assessment of responsibility. *Social Problems*, 1968, *16*(1), 3–19.

Schofield, W. *Psychotherapy: The Purchase of Friendship*, Englewood Cliffs, N.J.: Prentice-Hall, 1964.

Schopler, J and Bateson, N. The power of dependence. *Journal of Personality and Social Psychology*, 1965, *2*(2), 247–254.

Schopler, J. and Thompson, D. Role of attribution processes in mediating amount of reciprocity for a favor. *Journal of Personality and Social Psychology*, 1968, *10*(3), 243–250.

Schur, E. M. *Narcotic addiction in Britain and America*. Bloomington, Ind.: Indiana University Press, 1963.

Schur, E. M. *Crimes without victims*. Englewood Cliffs, N.J.: Prentice-Hall, 1965.

Schwartz, B. The social psychology of the gift. *American Journal of Sociology*, 1967, *73*(1), 1–11.

Sharoff, R. L. Character problems and their relationship to drug abuse. *American Journal of Psychoanalysis*, 1969, *29*(2), 186–193.

Sheehy, G. *Speed is of the essence*. New York: Pocket Books, 1971.

Slovenko, R. Psychiatry, criminal law, and the role of the psychiatrist. *Duke Law Journal*, 1963, *1963*(3), 395–426.

Snortum, J. R. Attitudes toward criminality as held by community residents, police officers, and prison inmates. *Proceedings of the*

References

Annual Convention of the American Psychological Association, 1971, *6*(1), 401–402.

Stoller, R. J. and Geertsma, R. H. The consistency of psychiatrists' clinical judgements. *Journal of Nervous and Mental Disease*, 1963, *137*, 58–66.

Storms, M. D. and Nisbett, R. E. Insomnia and the attribution process. *Journal of Personality and Social Psychology*, 1970, *16*(2), 319–328.

Sutter, A. G. Worlds of drug use on the street scene. In D. R. Cressey and D. A. Ward (Eds.) *Delinquency, crime, and social process*. New York: Harper and Row, 1969, Pp. 802–829.

Szasz, T. *Law, liberty, and psychiatry*. New York: Macmillan, 1963.

Szasz, T. *Psychiatric justice*. New York: Macmillan, 1965.

Tappan, P. W. Medical-legal concepts of criminal insanity. *Journal of Criminal Law and Criminology*, 1952, *43*, 333–334.

Thibaut, J. and Gruder, C. L. Formation of contractual agreements between parties of equal power. *Journal of Personality and Social Psychology*, 1969, *11*(1), 59–65.

Thibaut, J. W. and Kelley, H. H. *The Social Psychology of Groups*. New York: John Wiley, 1959.

Thomas, H. E. The dangerous offender. *Syracuse Law Review*, 1963, *14*(4), 576–585.

Thompson, T. and Pickens, R. Stimulant self-administration by animals: Some comparisons with opiate self-administration. *Federation Procedures*, 1970, *29*, 6–12.

189

References

Thompson, W. R. *A preface to urban economics*. Baltimore: John Hopkins Press, 1965.

Titmuss, R. M. *The gift relationship: From human blood to social policy*, New York: Pantheon Books, 1971.

Toch, H. *The social psychology of social movements*. Indianapolis: Bobbs-Merrill, 1965.

Towns, C. B. The peril of the drug habit. *Century Magazine*, 1912, *84*, 580–587.

Turner, J. F. C. and Fichter, R. (Eds.) *Freedom to build*. New York: Macmillan, 1972.

Vaillant, G. E. A twelve-year follow-up of New York addicts: I. The relation of treatment to outcome. *American Journal of Psychiatry*, 1966, *122*, 727–737.

Vaillant, G. E., Shapiro, L. N., and Schmitt, P. Psychological motives for medical hospitalization. *Journal American Medical Association*, 1970, *214*(9), 1661–1665.

Valins, S. Cognitive effects of false heartrate feedback. *Journal of Personality and Social Psychology*, 1966, *4*(4), 400–408.

Valins, S. The perception and labeling of bodily changes as determinants of emotional behavior. In P. Black (Ed.) *Psysiological correlates of emotion*. New York: Academic Press, 1970. Pp. 229–243.

VanGennep, A. *The rites of passage*. Chicago: University of Chicago Press, 1960.

VanRooyen, R. J. and Ziady, F. Hypokalaemic alkalosis following the abuse of purgatives. *South African Medical Journal*, 1972, *46*, 998–1003.

References

Vinar, O. Dependence on a placebo: A case report. *British Journal of Psychiatry*, 1969, *115*, 1189–1190.

Volkman, R. and Cressey, D. R. Differential association and the rehabilitation of drug addicts. *American Journal of Sociology*, 1963, *6*, 129–142.

Waelder, R. Psychiatry and the problem of criminal responsibility. *University of Pennsylvania Law Review*, 1952, *101*, 378–390.

Walster, E., Aronson, E., and Brown, Z. Choosing to suffer as a consequence of expecting to suffer: An unexpected finding. *Journal of Experimental Social Psychology*, 1966, *2*, 400–406.

Waltzer, H. A psychotic family—*folie a douze*. *Journal of Nervous and Mental Disease*, 1963, *137*(1), 67–75.

Watson, J. B. *Behaviorism*. (Rev. ed.) Chicago: University of Chicago Press, 1930.

Wechsler, H. The self-help organization in the mental health field. *Journal of Nervous and Mental Disease*, 1960, *130*, 297–314.

Wechsler, H. and Michael, J. A rationale of the law of homicide. *Columbia Law Review*, 1937, *37*, 701–761.

Weihofen, H. *The urge to punish*. New York: Farrar, Straus and Cudahy, 1956.

Weihofen, H. The definition of mental illness. *Ohio State Law Journal*, 1960, *21*(1), 1–16.

Weil, A. T., Zinberg, N. E., and Nelsen, J. M. Clinical and psychological effects of marihuana in man. *Science*, 1968, *162*, 1234–1242.

Weil, A. The natural mind. *Psychology Today*, 1972, *6*(5), 51–96.

191

References

Wenger, J and Einstein, S. The use and misuse of aspirin: A contemporary problem. *International Journal of Addictions*, 1970, *5*, 757–775.

Wertham, F. Psychoauthoritarianism and the law. *University of Chicago Law Review*, 1955, 22, 336–338.

Wexler, D. B. Token and taboo: Behavior modification, token economies, and the law. *California Law Review*, 1973, *61*(1), 81–109.

Whitehouse, F. A. Response to symbolic logic: The subtlety of interpersonal exchange. Proceedings of the 77th Annual Convention of the APA, 1969, *4* (Pt. 2), 775–776.

Whiting, J. W. M. Sorcery, sin, and the superego: A cross-cultural study of some mechanisms of social control. In M. R. Jones (Ed.) *1959 Nebraska Symposium on Motivation*. Lincoln: University of Nebraska Press, 1959.

WHO Expert Committee on Drug Dependence. *Sixteenth Report*. Geneva: World Health Organization Technical Report, Series No. 407, 1969.

Wilkins, L. T. Some sociologic factors in drug-addiction control. In D. M. Wilner and G. G. Kassebaum (Eds.) *Narcotics*. New York: McGraw-Hill, 1965. Pp. 140–156.

Winick, C. The psychology of juries. In H. Toch (Ed.) *Legal and criminal Psychology*. New York: Holt, Rinehart and Winston, 1961, Pp. 96–120.

Winick, C. Physician narcotic addicts. *Social Problems*, 1961, *9*(2), 174–186.

References

Yablonsky, L. *The tunnel back: Synanon.* New York: Macmillan, 1965.

Zilboorg, G. *Mind, medicine and man.* New York: Harcourt, Brace and Co., 1943.

Zimbardo, P. G. The psychology of police confessions. *Psychology Today*, 1967, *1*,(2), 17–27.

Zimbardo, P. and Ebbesen, E. B. *Influencing attitudes and changing behavior.* Reading, Mass.: Addison-Wesley, 1969.

Zinberg, N. and Robertson, J. *Drugs and the public.* New York: Simon and Schuster, 1972.

Zwerling, I. and Rosenbaum, M. Alcoholic addiction and personality. In S. Arieti (Ed.) *American handbook of psychiatry.* Vol. I. New York: Basic Books, 1959, Pp. 623–644.

Index

Index

Index

Index

Index

Index

Index

Carl N. Edwards is Assistant Clinical Professor of Psychiatry at the Tufts University School of Medicine and Senior Associate for Policy Planning and Research at the Justice Resource Institute. A former Harvard University Research Fellow and Lecturer on Social Relations, he has held teaching and research appointments at several universities in addition to serving major corporations, government agencies, and public institutions as a consultant in human dynamics and public policy. He is a frequent contributor to the literature on human dynamics, organizational behavior, and evaluation methodology, and is author of the forthcoming book *Human dynamics of change and challenge: A handbook for public policy and social change.*

The *Justice Resource Institute* is a Boston-based independent organization devoted to the research, development, and administration of innovative programs in criminal justice. *John A. Calhoun* is Executive Director of the Justice Resource Institute and former Director of the Boston Court Resource Project, Boston's pre-trial diversion program. He has been an active force in the creation and operation of numerous human service and criminal justice programs.